Buying and Selling a Business for Wealth

Kevin Uphill and Alex McMillan

Viva Books

New Delhi | Mumbai | Chennai | Kolkata | Bangalore | Hyderabad | Kochi

First Indian Edition 2009

VIVA BOOKS PRIVATE LIMITED

- 4737/23 Ansari Road, Daryaganj, New Delhi 110 002
  E-mail: vivadelhi@vivagroupindia.net, Tel. 42242200
- 76, Service Industries, Shirvane, Sector 1, Nerul, Navi Mumbai 400 706
  E-mail: vivamumbai@vivagroupindia.net, Tel. 27721273, 27721274
- Jamals Fazal Chambers, 26 Greams Road, Chennai 600 006
  E-mail: vivachennai@vivagroupindia.net, Tel. 28290304, 28294241
- B-103, Jindal Towers, 21/1A/3 Darga Road, Kolkata 700 017
  E-mail: vivakolkata@vivagroupindia.net, Tel. 22836381, 22816713
- 7, Sovereign Park Apartments, 56-58, K. R. Road, Basavanagudi, Bangalore 560 004
  E-mail: vivabangalore@vivagroupindia.net, Tel. 26607409, 26607410
- 101-102 Mughal Marc Apartments, 3-4-637 to 641, Narayanguda, Hyderabad 500 029
  E-mail: vivahyderabad@vivagroupindia.net, Tel. 27564481, 27564482
- First Floor, Beevi Towers, SRM Road, Kaloor, Kochi 682 018, Kerala
  E-mail: vivakochi@vivagroupindia.net, Tel: 0484-2403055, 2403056
- H. No. 12, P. B. Road, Near Arya Hospital, Rehabari, Guwahati 781 008
  E-mail: vivaguwahati@vivagroupindia.net, Tel: 0361-2735624

www.vivagroupindia.com

Published by arrangement with

Thorogood Publishers Limited
10-12 Rivington Street
London EC2A 3DU,
UK

ISBN-10: 81-309-1030-6
ISBN-13: 978-81-309-1030-7

Published by Vinod Vasishtha for Viva Books Private Limited, 4737/23, Ansari Road, Daryaganj, New Delhi-110 002. Printed and bound by Anand Sons, Delhi - 110 092.

Preface

Our aim in this book is to share the how, why and when of being a successful capitalist through buying and selling a business for wealth. If you currently own a business, or are thinking of starting or buying one, then this book is for you. Additionally, if you advise business owners this book may be useful.

Unless you are due one day to receive a large inheritance or win the national lottery for the vast majority of us building and selling our own business is the greatest opportunity that our society offers us to become financially free. Imagine having enough money invested that you need never worry again about paying the bills, being made redundant, taking a holiday where and when you want. Financial freedom gives you more opportunity to achieve life wealth in exploring opportunities other than working.

We provide an overview of the technical aspects of the process: the how. We have also examined the personal motivations, or the Big Adventure behind deals: the why. There are other books on the technicalities, but they ignore the fundamentally important aspect that delivering a business transaction is a means to an end. The why, the human story and motivations behind the deal are more important. Buying or starting a business and then selling it should make you financially wealthy, but it should also deliver life experience and time freedom.

We hope you enjoy the book, and achieving life wealth through a transaction.

Kevin Uphill

Acknowledgements and authors' experience

In writing this book we have included real stories of people who have achieved wealth through transactions and pulled on our and their combined experience. Kevin's experience comes from that of establishing and building a National UK-based professional practice (Avondale) that specializes in achieving transactions and life wealth. Alex's expertise comes from over 15 years as an executive coach, successful author, MBA and acknowledged expert in the field of entrepreneurship, and chairman of Club Entrepreneur. We have also pulled on the resources and experience of the many experts we know in the field, previous clients and our work colleagues. This book would not be complete without an acknowledgement of their help (you know who you are). A thank you to our respective families is also deserved for believing that we could author another book despite our already busy careers, and supporting us in the late nights this entailed.

The Authors

Kevin Uphill was born in the UK. After an early career in banking and financial services, he established Avondale in 1992 in his early twenties. From a two person professional practice the firm now has a national network and consults on over 100 transaction projects a year. He is a family man with one young daughter. He is the owner of a motor boat cruiser much to the family's dissent, a keen tri-athlete and marathon runner, interested historian and avid reader. **www.avondale.co.uk**

Alex McMillan is a Management Consultant and business author with a specific interest in entrepreneurs, who has set up businesses in both recruitment and training. He has initiated a company which offers job-hunting services via other people's Internet sites. He is building up this company for the purposes of selling for capital gain, applying all the principles in this book. **www.clubentrepreneur.co.uk**

Contents

chapter one Wealth creation

ONE Wealth creation

"Entrepreneurs are simply those who understand that there is little difference between obstacle and opportunity and are able to turn both to their advantage."

Niccolo Machiavelli

"If not us, who? If not now, when?"

John F. Kennedy

"He that waits upon fortune is never sure of a dinner."

Benjamin Franklin

Chapter focus

A look at the different ways that wealth is created so you can see which way is best for you and to put our proposal in context. We then put the case that wealth can be best created for business owners by selling their business.

- **Introduction**
- **Financial wealth accumulation plan**
- **How is wealth created?**
- **Why do people buy or sell a business?**
- **Why you should work on selling your business**
- **Summary**

Introduction

Obtaining wealth both financially and personally (abundance of happiness, job satisfaction, social contacts, good health, time freedom etc.) has always been a major part of our motivation. This is because it is generally our nature to seek beyond day-to-day survival to long term comfort, self-actualization and self-esteem. It is our contention that financial wealth can be efficiently created for business owners through buying (if you are not already an owner), adding value and then selling a business. We consider that buying is a better, safer and faster route to wealth than a start-up. We also believe that realizing a capital gain through a sale will usually achieve personal wealth far quicker than by profit accumulation over time.

Building up a business and selling it brings a rich and diverse range of experience, knowledge and contacts in addition to money. It also creates freedom to explore one's true capabilities and brings with it the thrill of winning in the face of adversity. The successful sale is the Gold Medal award. Most people spend their entire career creating wealth for other people. This is probably due to a lack of perceived opportunity, risk aversion and the drive for security in the form of a regular paycheck. The increasing pace of change in the business arena today has led to increasing opportunity for business venturers and decreasing security for employees. Many therefore see working for themselves as a preferred route.

In this chapter we outline some of the options available to create wealth. We ignore inherited or gifted wealth, as this is not creation. We then explain why the buying or starting, adding value and selling a business option has in our opinion the advantage. This chapter is aimed at the business owner or someone shortly to become such. The negotiation chapter will look at both positions of buying and selling a business. Even if you are just interesting in selling it is important to understand buyer tactics.

Financial wealth accumulation plan

What is financial wealth and is it possible to plan for it? Economic theory describes capital wealth as the means to live beyond the day-to-day work/earn cycle. That is you are no longer dependent on your direct input of labour to pay your way.

Wealth creation then is not so much about what you earn but about how much you save from what you earn and invest wisely. This goes some way to explain that in the UK and USA there is no real correlation between the wealthy and those with higher salaries. Those with higher salaries tend to spend more rather than accumulate wealth. A private pension is probably the commonest and most thought about route to such capital wealth. The concept is simple – accumulate enough of a capital sum to be able to stop, slow or choose a different work or lifestyle with income being derived from the interest/investment return on the capital with minimum risk. Well, at least that's the theory anyway, although many are now finding that, with volatile stock markets, pensions are not quite as assured as they had hoped. Despite this, pensions are a proven approach to capital wealth and this demonstrates in just one method that a plan to wealth is possible.

Most employees are on a simple wealth accumulation plan. They try to keep in regular employment until they are 65. In the meantime they target the biggest mortgage they can and continually chip away at it until 30 years plus later they have paid it off. Coupled with a good pension investment they should be secure with a non-labour dependent income when they are 65. A good plan if you love your work, there is a long term demand for your skills, if you are happy to wait until you are 65, if you trust that your pension scheme will not let you down (investments can go up as well as down), and if you keep your health into old age so as to avoid expensive care issues. It also assumes that, even if you love your work, you are happy to give it up totally when you are 65. A factor that invariably reduces other types of personal wealth discussed later.

There are other flaws. Firstly, few people are going to get secure work for their whole career. Secondly, the higher you get in management and the older, the fewer vacancies there are to get back to work once you are out. Thirdly, the day-to-day costs of living in a consumer world make saving increasingly difficult, particularly for those with one income and a young family. Fourthly, the Internet has enabled countries like India to take tens of thousands of jobs, like IT Software, away from us.

Pensions are a common route to wealth and accessible to most, although they do tend to take many years and they can usually only be enjoyed in old age. We believe it is also possible to plan wealth through other methods that are far quicker and offer a greater return. You have choices. It is a result of what you choose to do with your time. Wealth largely comes to those who plan for it. Those who acquire it without planning tend to lose it. Planning starts with where you are now and where you want or need to be. It starts with setting goals.

How is wealth created?

Wealth can be defined in both financial and personal terms. How you define it personally is subjective; however financial wealth is measurable and therefore accountable. In Britain at the beginning of the millennium there were recorded as being over 180,000 millionaires. This figure, adjusted for inflation, had steadily risen from 100,000 in 1996. Nearly half of this is attributable to rises in property values, but how have the rest done it? Below we have listed some of the ways:

Entrepreneurial

- Buy and sell a business
- Float a business (Michael Page/Recruitment)
- Property development/investment (Donald Trump)
- Start up your own business (Richard Branson, Sainsbury's)
- Float new venture, capital-backed venture (Lastminute.com)
- Franchising (many McDonalds restaurant owners)
- Network marketing (many Amway distributors)
- Invent something and patent it (James Dyson)
- Buying and selling shares (Warren Buffet)

Employment

- Stock option schemes in a star start-up (early Microsoft staff)
- Chief Executive of a major corporation (Jack Welch)
- Top city fund broker/lawyer/markets players

Entertainment

- Star, TV, arts, film or pop (Madonna)
- Sport, one that appeals to the masses (David Beckham)

Other

- Despot (Shah of Iran)
- Crime (Medellin Cartel, Mafia Bosses)
- Strike lucky (gambling, the National Lottery)

- Strike oil (Paul Getty)
- Inherited wealth (Royalty, Paul Getty the Fourth)
- Pensions and saving (retired employee)

We have not put in a named example for buying and selling a business. We can think of many but you probably will not have heard of them. This is because hundreds of people become wealthy through this route every day, but they or their business are not famous or in the media. This book might motivate you to put your name in this space. The alternative routes to wealth are listed for you to choose, or to choose not to become wealthy because it is, as we see it, your choice. Interestingly, entrepreneurship has several categories and is the one open to all of us with the inclination. It is also the category which gives us most control of our destiny, and according to Forbes produces the world's richest. Entrepreneurship is, therefore, apart from saving, one of the few ways open to plan for wealth without relying heavily on luck.

In addition, with the advent of the Internet, service industries and in particular conceptual and technology businesses, there are less barriers to business entry than at anytime in our history. Land was the key to wealth in early society, at a time when agriculture was the most important industry. Later, transportation such as shipping and the railways become key as new markets could be reached, and produce from the world brought back to Britain. Then came the advent of the industrial revolution meaning that efficiency in manufacturing process became the focus. Energy was next, starting with coal and then later oil-producing entrepreneurs such as John D. Rockefeller and John Paul Getty.

Wealth created by the early entrepreneurs was controlled by a very small percentage of the population. Establishing a business in manufacturing or oil, for example, meant the investment of large amounts of capital. Later, government policies distributed wealth to the masses as the economy grew. This in itself created larger markets of buyers, which in turn provided more opportunities for entrepreneurs. Post-war Britain saw new businesses launched, which today are household names. Marks & Spencer, Forte Hotels and Cadbury's started off as very small businesses and were developed over years to what they have become.

The latest development from a historic perspective is the Internet and other information technologies. This has already created a long list of millionaire entrepreneurs such as Jeff Bezos of Amazon. The key ingredient for our current age is more about creative ideas and marketing innovations using new technology. Small businesses increasingly are operating internationally. As the Internet and other technologies develop, so rapidly, more opportunities are made available to those that can see them and exploit the opportunities.

In Britain a proportion of the new wealthy have come from the recent technology bubble; however the majority have come from the small to middle-sized business market. They have built up successful ventures, earning good incomes and saving as they go along to then cap this off with a sale. For many the goal is a million, although most are happy to settle for less. In 2004 there were over 30 announced deals completed at £10 million plus in the UK, and this was despite a poor flotation (private to quoted) market. The majority of these successful owners are ordinary hardworking people. They did not invent a new operating system, win the lottery, inherit or invent a new technology. Most of them, when or if in the corporate world, did not make it as far as senior management. Most of them are not business graduates, chartered accountants, stockbrokers or experts. Most are ordinary people who simply chose the entrepreneurial route, took and managed the risks and worked hard at getting it right.

Why do people buy or sell a business?

Businesses today operate in a fast moving market place, which has had a dramatic effect on the way they function. It is very rare for an enterprise to maintain the initial status quo, and nor should they aim to. Businesses change, expand or contract in balance with the current economy. It is this constant change that has made mergers, acquisitions, sales and takeovers commonplace in today's global commercial environment. The competitive pressure and increasingly legislative environment we live in makes both sales of businesses and acquisitions attractive. Whilst one owner exits, relieving the burden of competition, the trade buyer benefits from an increase in market domination and economies of scale easing competition or legislative pressures.

Sales of businesses in the small to middle-sized market are much more common. Owners seek shorter periods of stewardship so they can explore other options, ambitions or careers. Trade sales are further increased with a reduction in family succession. In other words, handing the business down to the family is far less common. Young adults have more choice today and typically do not want to run the family business. The business might require skills they just don't have.

Currently (2006) in the UK, a taxation benefit called taper relief further encourages entrepreneurs to seek a sale. This is an Inland Revenue allowance, which significantly reduces capital gains tax on the sale of business assets.

People buy a business to:

- Avoid the risks of a start up.
- Increase market share. Acquisition is usually easier than organic growth.
- Increase profits or shareholder value.
- Secure products, staff and knowledge.
- Create synergies or economies of scale in the operation.
- Buy a job.
- Buy, build and sell on.
- Enable a new management to seize an opportunity they see to do better than the current owners.

People sell a business:

- To realize the capital value of the business for the owner's benefit, or to provide capital for either a new or an existing venture.
- To seek other opportunities as the present management has developed the business as far as they are able or want to.
- To benefit from a market development that makes it advantageous to sell, such as a technological development or high value being attached to the business.
- Because of an inability to develop a business further due to a lack of capital.
- For a lifestyle change.
- To retire or because of illness with no succession.

Why you should work on selling your business

If you look at rich lists (www.forbes.com) in the UK or rest of the world, it is clear that many of the big financial wealth accumulators come from the ranks of entrepreneurs. The business owners that founded a company and took it to international size are the ones that become famous. More numerous but less commonly known are the many people who never achieved any level of fame but nonetheless achieved significant financial wealth. Whilst there are risks to building a business specifically for sale, we contend that, if these are managed and a sale is planned, then risks are considerably reduced and one of the most accessible, fastest and likely routes to financial and personal wealth is being followed.

There are many founding entrepreneurs who have achieved wealth whose motivation was often not capital gain although they achieved it, such as Walt Disney. Money therefore, need not be the only goal to the entrepreneur. The satisfaction of seeing an idea or concept turn to profit is often the main motivator; in other words, self-actualization mixed with financial reward.

The pros and cons of wealth creation through buying and selling a business

Advantages	Disadvantages
Unlike most of the other methods there is no or little real barrier to entry.	Seed capital or purchase deposit required.
Finance for going concern accessible.	Entrepreneurial risk and leadership don't suit everybody.
Relies less on talent than say arts, sports.	Investment in intangible asset as opposed to say property.
Fame is a choice – if very successful, one most choose to avoid	Investment not immediately realizable as opposed to say stocks and shares.
Challenge and satisfaction of achievement are substantial.	Needs very careful and time-consuming assessment of value.
Timescale is short in comparison to say pensions and saving or stock investments.	Risk of bankruptcy.
Experience, knowledge and contacts developed through growing a business very personally rewarding.	Hardwork sometimes
Independence, freedom and master of your own destiny.	Requires common sense and commercial acumen (although both can be learnt).

Summary

Starting or buying, adding value and then selling a business is statistically the most likely route available today to achieve significant capital wealth. There are no longer the historical barriers to entry. Quite the opposite – there is a myriad of advice and encouragement organizations and Government support schemes. When you look at the alternative of uncertain career and a long wait until you receive a questionable pension, entrepreneurship really is the attractive option so long as you manage the risks. If you already own a business you are half way there.

By opting not just for profit, but also to run a business for shareholder value or capital growth in the value of your business you achieve a double whammy. Not only do you enjoy the profits as you go along, but you bank a reserve. The whole process can also provide personal fulfilment, fun along the way, contacts and building your self-esteem.

CASE STUDY (SOURCE: AVONDALE GROUP)

NICHE BUILDING CONTRACTOR S.EAST
T/O £1.1M, NP £253,000 **SOLD JUNE 2004**

At one time or another many of us have flicked through the pages of Country Life and gazed at the beautiful properties and their opulent surroundings, daydreaming of owning such a place perhaps. Nick Newton went a step better and spent his working life around such houses. Nick owned and ran a specialist building firm which renovated and refurbished listed buildings, both privately owned and those run by charitable trusts, in the South East. He worked hard to build up his business and established a reputation for quality craftsmanship. After almost twenty years Nick found himself at a crossroads. For some time he had been struggling to keep up as a smaller business with the increasing number of new regulations in the building industry.

He started to carefully plan his exit route. After years working in other people's homes, his dream was to build his own house in a small UK village in Kent. Using the craftsmen he employed and trusted Nick fulfilled his dream and built his house. He then contacted specialist Broker, Avondale, to find him a purchaser for the business. Nick's main objectives were that he received as much of the consideration as possible on day one and that there was no prolonged handover.

Through careful research a number of purchasers were found. One in particular already owned a specialist commercial building firm and had specifically been looking for another niche building contractors to add diversity, and to provide economies of scale. Nick's business therefore was a perfect synergy. A deal was done.

Nick has now purchased a smaller service company to keep him occupied.

"Today the greatest single source of wealth is between your ears."

Brian Tracy

chapter two Business owner – Who dares wins...

TWO Business owner – Who dares wins…

"What would life be if we had no courage to attempt anything?"

Van Gogh

"One does these things because one has a certain nature. One cannot get away from fate. If a person does not fulfil his nature, he will lead a frustrated life and be unhappy. If it involves him in fear he will just have to put up with it."

Sir Francis Chichester

"The best time to invest is when it is extremely difficult to summon up the courage to do so."

Jim Slater

Chapter focus

To outline the skills, attitude and personality you will need to be an owner/investor/manager that can successfully add value to and sell a business for capital gain.

- **Introduction**
- **The owner/manager profile**
- **Risk management**
- **Passion for profits**
- **Improving skills**
- **Making it work**
- **Releasing the owner/manager investor within**
- **Summary**

Introduction

Buying, merging, establishing and building up a business is a wealth-fulfilling activity, particularly if ultimately a sale for capital gain is to be sought. It is also very entrepreneurial. This means, before it's undertaking, we believe it is vital to understand the attributes, responsibility and role of the successful owner/manager. There are many elements to the successful owner/manager and therefore all we attempt in this chapter is to provide a snapshot for the new potential entrepreneur and a reminder for the existing. Everyone ultimately has his or her style, ideas, strengths and weaknesses. Some are naturals and some have to work at it or learn it.

If you have bought this book to find out more about selling a business, then it may be helpful to skip this chapter. You probably already know what it means to be an owner/manager and have already made the decision to exit at some point.

The owner/manager profile

What are the attributes of the successful owner/manager and have you got what it takes?

There are many tests on the Internet that will help tell you, although if you have to take a test you probably don't have the self-confidence right now to succeed. Running a business requires self-confidence and risk-taking.

The big difference between an owner and a corporate manager is that although many of the decisions are the same, for the owner/manager each decision is a risk-all; after all, it is now their money. We have seen corporate managers who have become owner/managers become totally risk-taking and some totally risk-averse. Both are approaches that will usually end in failure. The middle route of carefully managed risk is usually the most effective.

One reason many choose to stay employees is the feeling of security and control they believe employment offers; however in an uncertain economic world redundancies and short-term employment are common. This means employment can be high risk, particularly as often the employee's destiny is in the hands of others. Employees often have no say or control on their future. Many entrepreneurs see this and although it means leaving the crowds and joining the few they would rather have the security that they decide their destiny and control their future. For them the argument is that employment is the risky investment. At least as an owner/manager their success and failure is in their hands. There are of course disadvantages and different stresses. One owner/manager we know says the change is like getting a salary review, up or down, at the end of every day. This creates immense pressure, and many find it difficult to switch off as a result. The successful usually adapt their belief system to develop protective philosophies to cope. These vary from person to person but might include 'it's only money', 'it's the winning that counts but not at the expense of my health'.

Attributes: Self-confidence, managed risk-takers, control focus and adaptable belief system

If you have had a business career, or your parents ran a small business, then you will have a head-start as an owner/manager. Yet the whole point of entrepreneurship and achieving capital wealth through this route is that it is open to anybody. A range of different talents can all be put to use in the right situation and opportunity. It is not really a matter of can you do it, or have you got the skill. It is more about matching your skills and profiles to an opportunity that you can add value to. We are all talented. The successful are the ones that match their specific talents and motivations to opportunity, i.e. they think about how to be in the right place and at the right time. Whatever your life situations and experiences, they have shaped who you are today. You are unique and as such will see things that others don't. This gives you unique advantages and opportunities.

To see opportunities that others have missed you sometimes need to take a different perspective. So often business innovations have come from people who are not part of the current way of doing things. They tend to ask more questions, from their ignorance. Why do you do things this way, why do you buy that way? When that question gets ums and errs, something that indicates that the person or client has habitually done it that way, you have an opportunity. How could it be done better? If we repeat a task we write a piece of mental software called a habit and tend to just do it on automatic, yet these habits once formed are not updated or reviewed usually, unless change is forced upon us.

As economies evolve, markets change, old ones die off and new ones are created. Predicting these trends is important if you are to lead a business. Smaller firms generally can be more flexible than their larger counterparts, enabling them to capitalize quickly on opportunities.

Attributes: Focus on how to be in the right place at the right time, and ask how to do it better

Successful owner/managers are typically strong-minded determined people with bags of self-confidence and a clear monetary focus. This does not mean that they are arrogant, believing they have every skill. You need to be prepared to work long hours and fit family commitments around the business. You need to be stubborn, disciplined and see things through to success, however arduous the journey. It is an advantage if you naturally like networking and meeting people, because you are constantly in search of suppliers, people who can do things for you, customers, staff etc.

Attributes: Monetary focus, strong-minded, disciplined, networkers, interested in people, stubborn, determined and hard-workers

Most successful owner/managers are practical and action-orientated. It is important to understand that plans are just plans unless they are put into action. Even then plans need to be adaptable to react to external pressures. A planner and 'doer' are therefore positive attributes, particularly if combined with flexibility.

Attributes: Planners who are flexible, action orientated and practical

We have established that owner/managers require confidence and strong minds. Often, however, these attributes can go hand in hand with arrogance (thinking you are better than you are). The danger of arrogance is that it results in poor listening and a lack of receptivity. An 'I know that' or 'I don't need to know' attitude as a result of arrogance can be very dangerous to the entrepreneur. It can result in a failure to take, seek or understand advice, or over-confidence. In particular, a danger is underestimating the market or competition.

Successful owner/managers are typically listeners who respect others' opinions and choose the good bits. They are receptive to ideas, knowledge and advice. The really strong ones usually also have a strong market orientation and 'listen' to what the market is telling them. They also learn from their mistakes, rather than dwelling on them and letting them affect their commitment.

William Shakespeare sums it up with this quotation from his play 'As You Like It': "The fool doth think he is wise, but the wise man knows himself to be a fool."

Attributes: Listeners and learners who believe in knowledge and help

You need to be able to motivate yourself and others. You need inspiration followed by perspiration. The inspiration has got to be researched and tested. The perspiration must be relentless.

Attributes: Motivation, leadership and passion

Many may be surprised to see that high intelligence has not featured as an attribute. This is perhaps because it is not a prerequisite and can be a disadvantage. High intelligence can lead to over-processing when making decisions (procrastination), rather than relying on instinct. We have met several self-made millionaires who did not understand a balance sheet, but they understood cash and had a lot of practical common sense. Know your strengths and weaknesses. Capitalize on your strengths, work on your weaknesses.

Attributes: Common sense, capitalize on strengths, work on weaknesses

Risk management

Do you see risk or opportunity? The successful owner/manager sees both, as two sides of the same coin. Probably the most recognized trait of entrepreneurs is the ability to take risks. Many see this as the biggest barrier to becoming an entrepreneur because they feel risk-adverse. However, being an entrepreneur is not so much about being brave as taking carefully managed risks, more interestingly a trait associated with the risk-adverse. Risk, when it creates fear, can hold you back or even destroy you. Yet when risk produces analysis and projection, you can manage it, even turn it to advantage. If you read the biographies of famous entrepreneurs from Bill Gates and Richard Branson to Aristotle Onassis and Henry Ford, you will realize that after they saw an opportunity they thoroughly investigated any potential future risk and made plans how to deal with them if and when they should come up.

Entrepreneurs take risks, and their motivations to do this vary a great deal. The fact that they take risks does not mean that they are fearless of things going wrong. On the contrary: fear makes them want to minimize or spread the risk. There are two key emotions that can, when taking risks, erode your success if they are not managed and disciplined. Fear tends to encourage people to follow the crowd, for safety. This is not usually a winning formula that will get you ahead of the crowd. The second is greed, which can lead to over-stretching yourself or being over-optimistic. Realism and analysis are essential.

When you have nothing to lose any business risk is no big deal. Many of the world's greatest entrepreneurial successes came following adversity. People are made redundant at age 55, have no assets behind them and cannot secure new employment. Your worst fears have already been materialized, you can only move up. Your time is effectively free. If you have a small capital stake, it might not be enough to retire on but it could get you started in your own business. If you did not use it immediately in this way, then probably it would whittle down to nothing over the next few months and then you would go into debt. So adversity can become a great advantage and opportunity for you.

If you have a big house with an equally big mortgage on it, kids at private schools and have a regular executive position that keeps you afloat, then you are unlikely, however much you hate the job and have a desire for your own enterprise, to make the leap. The leap is usually made for such people when they are made redundant. Their first instinct is to panic and do everything possible to get another job fast.

On the other hand you already own your own business and are caught up in the day to day survival, cash flow management and the pursuit of profit. If this is the case, changing your focus to selling for capital gain actually reduces the risk. It will take all your eggs out of one basket. The same applies for a start-up operation.

We see four types of people:

1 Optimistic, you think every idea is going to be a great success.

2 Optimistic, but consider the downside before pursuing.

3 Pessimistic, but prepared to be convinced.

4 Pessimistic, sees more danger than reward in everything.

The ideal entrepreneurs or owner/managers are a B or a C. A's tend to do all the wrong things and learn the hard way. D's never get going with anything, and watch as others progress. Successful business people manage risk. They do not overcome the fear of risk or avoid taking risks.

The successful owner/manager will seek opportunities, and accept and manage risk

Passion for profit

Many people when they become self-employed say, "I like golf, interior design, cooking, cycling, sport", or whatever it is and focus on that as what they want to run a business in. They already have a passion for their hobby in life. This can result in a very successful formula if the timing is right because of the huge passion people bring to the product. However, we have noticed that the timing needs to be right and more often than not this approach usually results in an owner-managed lifestyle business – it makes a living but the owner works hard to achieve it.

Our observations of the truly successful owner/managers, particularly those we have seen sell out, are that they have limited emotional connection with their product. Their passion is more likely to be the business and business excellence. By making business their hobby it has the effect of focusing them on the business and not just the trade they wish to pursue. Because it becomes their hobby they don't mind working hard at it and actually enjoy it, which increases their motivation long-term.

If you make business excellence your hobby, than you can do whatever you like. This will also move your focus from what you want to do, to looking for what people want from you and are willing to pay money for.

The pragmatic realize it is not so much what they are doing but what they can do with it. You can make money out of cleaning drains. Your focus needs to be on the money not the drains. Step outside of what you think you want to do, that lifestyle job, more to the enjoyment of actually running the business. Rule number one, the main focus is to get cash from the customer. Rule number two is getting and satisfying more customers. Rule number three is selling more to your customers. Rule number four is keeping your cost as low as possible so as to maximize profit. All business at the end of the day comes down to the simple equation Sales minus Costs equals Profit. Obvious, but it is amazing how many small and big businesses are not working this equation.

Make business your hobby.

Improving skills

Business success is practical and thus learnt more through experience than the classroom. That is not to suggest that there is any less learning to do, just don't expect to get a certificate for it! Lessons in business life are usually learnt quicker when accompanied by an unpleasant experience. You learn fast what does not work and can move on. Every entrepreneur biography at the back of this book will give you examples of this. Give a new business graduate a random object and say, "Sell this to me" and you will see how novice their skills are. Usually they will describe the feature of the object you gave them and keep talking about it. Ask the same challenge to anyone who has worked in a shop and they will typically have a much better answer. They have been in the real world and know that people do not do what is logical and expected. They have learnt that you have to listen rather than talk to gather key information on the customer. They will probably start with a question about you, rather than the object to be sold for example.

At the end of the day customers control business direction. This is the first law of business. There are other laws that must be obeyed covering a myriad of areas from controlling accounts to workforce management, and creating effective operating systems. Obey the laws and you will prosper. Look at the dot.com bust in 2001 to see what happened when these laws were ignored and greed took over. A major technological shift changes the way we do business, but the bust shows that it does not change the fundamental laws.

Successful owner/managers actively seek to become expert business people and to understand the laws of business. They read books, join networks, take advice and seek knowledge and training. They stay up to date with the latest trends and theories and adapt what works to their business. They are constantly seeking ideas old or new that can help grow their business.

We suggest the simplest, cheapest and one of the more effective ways is to continually read the books of successful entrepreneurs. They are all adventure stories anyway and are a very relaxing way to improve your skills. A large company, when planning marketing, establishes the budget and analyzes the various choices available. An owner/manager looks for innovative ideas to market his/her business without a budget, using the resources that are around, constantly looking until a way is found.

Successful entrepreneurs seek continuous personal improvement and ideas.

Making it work

Entrepreneurship is a practical skill. Ideas, even good ideas, are quite common; the real skill is in implementing them. Have you ever felt in your employment that you could do a better job than your bosses? Yet you were experienced enough to know that putting forward bright ideas risked your position, so you kept them to yourself. Well, when you have your own business we are really going to see how good your ideas are. You may find this scary on reflection.

The really clever business managers are those that nurture ideas from the staff and seriously listen to them. When you own the business you will not be concerned where the idea comes from if it puts profit in your pocket. You will also not be concerned so much with surviving company politics. However, your staff will, and you have to manage that. If a staff member is not performing in a large employer, managers often tolerate it, not wanting to let someone go. In your own business this is cash out of your salary on a daily basis.

There are lots of ways to implement yours and your team's ideas and get things done as an owner/manager. Obviously you may still be able to do it yourself but not if you cost yourself effectively; this means that delegation skills are paramount. The difficulty is that many owners started or are thinking of starting their own business because they want control and believe that nobody can do it better than them. This belief will lead to very long hours or a thwarted business. The best way is to spend time working on the business and really effectively mastering project and change management and delegation. These areas alone could fill volumes of text books so we will not go into too much detail. However, here are some tips:

- Remember, "plans are just that unless they rapidly deteriorate into action" (Peter Drucker – Management Guru).
- When you delegate it is your responsibility to track progress.
- A bad idea implemented well will be more effective than a good idea implemented badly.
- In the modern respect consider employees' culture; ask them how to get things done, listen and give them control and accountability to get things done. It may not be done exactly your way. It may be done better or worse, but it gets done. It also creates a more loyal workforce who feels their opinions are valued and make a difference.

There are times when you need to work in, as opposed to on, your business. You need to be in touch with the shop floor, that is where it all happens. If you just grow and delegate, that is, work **on** not **in** your business, you can lose touch with what is happening (Ivory Tower syndrome). Michael Marks, the co-founder of Marks & Spencers would even be seen sweeping a shop floor after they were a major household company. Richard Branson talks directly to his customers and staff all the time. Sainsbury's senior managers will be found in all parts of their operations.

Plan and then carry out action with a practical approach, an involved team and effective delegation. Stay in touch from the ground level up with what is really happening in your business.

Releasing the owner/manager investor within

As an owner/manager you are in business for yourself; you should not be in the 'selling your time for money' equation. You are in the leverage game, leveraging your ideas and efforts through a business, other people and opportunities to make some real money. Employees work a month for a secure payment at the end of it. As a business owner you should think investment, long-term and capital gain. Employees measure their level of success or status by their salary. Owner/manager investors measure their success by their wealth. They have people on salaries building up their wealth for them.

The owner/manager is in effective control of a commercial undertaking. The role should not be immediately confused with that of manager. Managers organize and co-ordinate businesses. Some also have effective control and ultimate responsibility. Many managing directors are, either by shareholding or by appointment of the shareholders, manager entrepreneurs.

Owner/managers have the final responsibility for a business. The buck stops with them. Their leadership, vision, strategy, ideas, bravery and risk management determine the success or failure of a business. Many will contend this is not fair as external factors also influence a businesses future. This is true but it is the entrepreneur's responsibility to either react or, better still, anticipate and embrace these uncertain external factors, whether they are people, competitors or social and economic factors. The role of the owner/manager is therefore exciting, challenging and rewarding. It is also very hard because whether the entrepreneur realizes or accepts it, they have no excuse for failure, only responsibility for success. We have listed below some of the key responsibilities of the owner/manager as we see it.

In the business the ability to:

- Develop a clear vision and strategy map
- Get others to follow this vision and map (it is enough that others follow the vision: they do not have to share it)
- Clearly adapt the map as matters progress
- Work on the map and the business not in it (i.e. to delegate where possible the actual job of work and to concentrate on the map, vision and growth)
- Look at the grand map whilst being aware of what is really happening on the shop floor (i.e. avoid ivory tower syndrome)
- Accept, take and manage risk
- Talk to customers, listen to and understand their needs, markets and trends
- See ahead, anticipate and innovate
- Constantly seek and make deals (not just in the early stages of a business)
- Continuously spot or create opportunities (to see the options)

- Nurture, encourage and acknowledge ideas from staff and others
- Seek and find cash (also to manage it well or get others to do this)
- Provide clear leadership, even in panic situations
- Choose conflict over harmony (if tough decisions need to be made the willingness to make them for the good of the business)
- Focus on the important and be decisive
- Set and focus on goals
- Invest, speculate and accumulate

Ask, 'How can I make the business better?' every day.

Summary

In summary, not everyone will have all of these skills, attributes and focuses, many will have different strengths, however the above represents, we hope, a basic insight into some of the characteristics we have seen from our experience required to build a successful venture and sell it for a capital gain.

"That some should be rich shows that others may become rich, and hence is just encouragement to industry and enterprise."
Abraham Lincoln

chapter three Why sell? – Looking at the big picture

THREE Why sell? – Looking at the big picture

"… and suddenly find – at the age of fifty, say – that a whole new life has opened before you, filled with things you can think about, study, or read about…it is as if a fresh sap of ideas and thoughts was rising in you."

Agatha Christie

"The best way to predict the future is to invent it."

Alan Kay

"I wasted time and now doth time waste me."

William Shakespeare

Chapter focus

To examine right from the start the personal motivations involved for building up and selling a business.

- **Introduction**
- **Why sell – your future?**
- **Life cycles- what next?**
- **The five types of wealth**
- **The eternal entrepreneur**
- **The sale proceeds**
- **Retreat and think**

Introduction

You might be surprised to see 'Why sell?' as Chapter 3 and so early on in the book. We believe, however, that it is vital to understand where you want to be right from the start. A sale may have been decided upon in a larger company by the board for strategic reasons; the owner/manager however is often the board in entirety, and his or her strategy to exit may be less clear. Traditionally, owner/manager sales have been for retirement or perhaps ill health. Today, this is changing. Increasingly owner/managers are selling to change their lifestyle without age or health featuring in the decision.

This chapter is aimed at the owner/manager or potential entrepreneur to explore why lifestyle is becoming as much a part of the decision to sell as business strategy. It will also be useful to those considering starting a new business to focus on the end game right from the start. There will always be strategic business reasons to sell. These might include the right offer, increasing competition, changing trends, or lack of capital, but what about personal motivations? Our aim in this chapter is to help owners to establish a clear personal motivation for a sale right from the beginning and plan for their future. Some of the advice is obvious but often forgotten in the excitement of a potential sale. This is probably because the focus is on delivering the deal, rather than counting cash not yet earned. However, this is flawed...if you know clearly where and why you want to be somewhere the journey is easier to make.

Why sell? – your future

"If you can count your money, you don't have a billion dollars."
J. Paul Getty

Money will not bring you happiness but it can make your misery more comfortable. There is a point in life when making money should be a priority. There is also a point to be reached where making money should cease to be the main goal. Paul Getty's biography shows that he had a billion dollars but did not have the other types of wealth, discussed later, that comprise happiness. The question therefore is: when is your financial wealth enough? You need to ask, when, how or even should you capitalize on your business asset to enable you to do other things and if so what?

You probably started a business because you wanted to be the boss. You wanted control, recognition and money. You also probably started a business around a job you enjoyed and were good at. That job became the business. You made it a success by being passionate, enjoying getting the deal, the challenge of creation and thinking big. You mixed this with determination, hard work and persevering through obstacles along the way.

Success produces a mature business. This means you have probably stopped doing 'the job'. Now you are running the business, designing systems, dealing with personnel, financial and legal issues, handling red tape and day-to-day management. It seems the business is controlling you and you have a boss again after all, in the form of your customers, staff, accountants and the government. The challenge of creation has also gone.

Of course the right answer would be to bring in management, but that would contradict the very reason for going it alone and starting a business in the first place. Didn't you say when you started that you wanted control of your destiny and to be beholden to no one? Besides, you can't delegate. No one does it as well as you or cares as much. They are just not as motivated or committed as you.

You are financially doing well and business is growing but the stakes are getting a bit high. The bank is asking you to put your house back on the line for continued support. You have been there ten years ago when you started so you are nervous to go through that pressure again. You decide it is time to sell.

Okay, so the above may not exactly be you but it is highly typical of many of the cases we see. Most people think of selling for retirement and ill health reasons. These reasons are still common, however the reality is much more complicated and there are a whole host of reasons why people choose to sell their business. Typically these include both strategic business and personal reasons, often being a mixture, including:

Lack of succession

The family business is not dead, but it has declined. Many entrepreneurs' sons or daughters seem today reluctant to get involved in the family concern. Perhaps because they have often been afforded a better education than the founder and therefore they see a broader perspective.

Perhaps also increasingly it is because the second generation are unable to afford to take the business on and match what a strategic trade buyer may value the business at. The first generation doesn't know how long they are going to live and they need to maximize their return after all, and giving it away to the family may not seem that attractive. Perhaps there is a further unspoken reason – the second generation don't want the comparison with the first. Can they do as well? They also recall the complaining done by their parents about the hours spent and the stress involved. Do they want this?

To combine with reduction of family succession, often there is also a lack of logical second tier management to take on the business. We have noticed that indeed this is one of the commonest drivers, although it is rarely identified directly by the owner. The business works with them there, but they are unable to let go or effectively delegate, or conversely the cost of second tier management that would enable this is prohibitive. Either way a strategic crossroads can be reached. Sell, or take the plunge and bring in expensive people and place the business under management. The 'under management' route is at first appealing but it creates no liquidity for the owner/manager seeking an exit. Also, will the second tier now promoted to a first do as good a job, particularly with their salaries now cutting the profit margin?

Capitalizing on their assets

Many owners have a high value in their business and without a sale, it is capital locked up. The sale can create personal liquidity or capital wealth enabling more choice and freedom in retirement or, more often than not these days, semi-retirement. A main focus of this book is to get new or current owners to see how they can make their businesses an asset that can deliberately be capitalized. In other words, growing and developing a business to sell for capital wealth as a primary motivator, rather than the traditional just 'work for profit' focus that seems to exist in the small and mid markets.

Benefits and synergy as part of a larger business

People buy companies because they offer growth, diversification, synergy and economies of scale. Trade buyers in particular will benefit. Many of these aspects are logical for the business as well. As part of something larger with low costs, the business is leaner and more competitive, more likely to survive. Many sellers recognize this and realize when it is time to let their baby go. Perhaps this thought process is combined with the personal desire to achieve liquidity, often mixed with the private thought that building it up was more fun than running it. Time to let the corporate take it from here.

Under capitalization

Typically this goes hand in hand with the above, but it may be that the existing owner/manager's resources are not enough to take the business to the next stage. Yet if businesses don't grow, generally they die. If there are insufficient assets in the business to enable finance to be leveraged, development can become stunted. Time to sell. Just because one owner lacks resource, it does not mean another will. Often corporate buyers have the confidence and money to take the smaller company and make it fly.

Life cycles – what next?

"Every exit is an entry somewhere else."

Tom Stoppard

Running a business is only one cycle of our careers. Before that we were an employee, and we are free to be an entrepreneur or an employee again if we so wish. The days of joining a company, staying there for 45 years and then retiring are gone, so why should a business be for life? We all have various needs, which change as we progress through life. People are focused on retiring and the very word conjures up an end. We believe it is a better philosophy to think in terms of changing cycles. By doing this we can seek new cycles and embrace them, rather than fear them out of conservatism.

Plan ahead now and you can manage a smooth transition into the next cycle of your life. After all, is this not what happens in your business? Different plans, priorities and objectives are set. Products, competition, staff, mission statements and goals change. Why not personally think of a mission statement for your next personal cycle and perhaps the one after that?

Abraham Maslow, one of the early researchers on motivation, classified the hierarchy of human needs as follows. The first two he considered basic and the other three he considered higher needs.

1 Physiological needs: food, water, shelter and clothing.
2 Security needs: safety, regular income and financial freedom.
3 Social needs: relationships, partner, family and friends.
4 Esteem needs: recognition and achievement.
5 Self-actualization: fulfilling one's potential.

It is interesting that by achieving financial security you only reach level 2. For your next cycle there is plenty of scope! In fact the danger is that fulfilment of needs 3, 4 and 5 might actually be reduced having sold your business. This is because in many cases the owner/manager's self-esteem is actually derived from his or her status and position as the boss. Remove this and you can end up feeling empty and demotivated.

An owner/manager sale requires both business strategic planning and personal planning. The successful exiting owner/manager will give much thought and planning early on to their personal, emotional and self-needs. Questions you could ask might be:

1 Who am I?
2 What motivates me?
3 What motivates my partner or family?
4 What would now give me great satisfaction?
5 Do I have a clear plan?
6 Putting money aside, what is my perfect job/lifestyle?

The five types of wealth

"Wealth is not his that has it, but his who enjoys it."

Benjamin Franklin

Often in business a one 'right approach' is advocated, usually the accounting one that ignores the core of a business, 'its people'. This approach often satisfies one need whilst creating another challenge. For most owners and their advisers the sale seems to be only about achieving financial wealth. We however, believe a sale should be about more than this. It should be about achieving:

- Financial wealth
- Relationship wealth
- Health wealth
- Time wealth
- Purpose wealth

Financial wealth

This is the easiest to measure. We think the benchmark goal for everybody is having enough assets that produce a monthly income, inflation linked, to equal your 'chosen' monthly expenditure. This should include a pension provision. At this crucial point you have achieved time wealth. Yet so many go on accumulating financial wealth that they don't need or have a real use for and lose this time. They either really enjoy what they do, or are on a treadmill and don't know how to get off. Perhaps they are insecure and can only think of hoarding more gold, or lack imagination as to what else to do. If you absolutely love your work with a passion, continue doing it. If you don't, ask yourself what you would love to do?

Relationship wealth

Entrepreneurs work long hours and perhaps it is time to spend more time with the family. Having financial freedom and nobody to share life with can be a very lonely, albeit a comfortable existence. For many of us our social relationships actually come from work. Suddenly these are cut and something needs to be put in its place.

Health wealth

It is interesting yet sad to note how many people we have met that spend their life pursuing financial security for their old age, whilst ignoring and often reducing their health wealth, perhaps through stress, bad diet, excessive drinking and lack of exercise. If you do not look after your health wealth you may never get to enjoy your financial wealth.

The advice in a typical doctor's surgery is simple and works. Plan ahead and take action to avoid problems. Spend time on your health. Eat fresh fruit and vegetables. Drink plenty of water and exercise regularly. Do not smoke and be moderate in drinking alcohol.

Time wealth

Now you have it, what to do with it? This is perhaps the most important question facing the selling owner. Many who retire are only too keen to replace all their previous long hours of work with relaxation and freedom. Running a small business is very time-consuming: managing staff, cash flow, administration, selling, training etc. To start each week without any of these chores can be quite motivating in itself. Very quickly though, however luxurious your home is, most of us will become very bored without something to do.

You should in reality be spoilt for choice. But as you have been running a business in a certain industry for the last several years your horizons may have become limited. You need to explore all the choices open to you. What other dreams did you have? For example:

- Write a novel(s)
- Flying lessons
- Learn to play an instrument
- Visiting friends in far away places
- Develop a new hobby or interest
- Consultancy to other business people
- Voluntary work helping undeveloped countries grow their economies
- Build a boat
- Travel and see some places you have always wanted to
- Sail around the world

Purpose wealth

It is a natural motivation to produce something of value for other people. We do this in our work, whatever it is, in some way contributing to the betterment of society. We also do this by bringing up children. We need to feel useful, add value and give to others.

The eternal entrepreneur

> *"Money was never a big motivation for me, except as a way to keep score. The real excitement is playing the game."*
>
> **Donald Trump**

For many, particularly younger owner/managers a sale can be an excellent way to achieve a sabbatical (rest) before starting again with financial security behind them. The challenge of creating a new business is often more appealing to serial entrepreneurs than running an established one. The wise will 'bank' a reserve; allocate a certain amount of money to a new project and stick to that allocation. If you are looking to start again with a new venture be aware of any non-compete clause (typically for three years) that you will have signed on sale. Remember, you have just got all your eggs out of one basket so, if you do start a business again, banking a reserve diversifies your portfolio.

There is an alternative to starting a new venture. Larger companies have increasingly realized the value of employing flexible entrepreneurs to expand their operations; so another opportunity exists. Working for the buyer could be an attractive opportunity so long as you can deal with the challenge of not being your own boss. In this case an outright exit need not be sought. Buyers tend to prefer the acquisition of a controlling interest, however they are also sometimes attracted by the idea of the previous owner having a continued stake. It gives them confidence in their investment.

For the exiting owner retaining a minority shareholding could lead to a future bonus perhaps from a trade sale or floatation in the future. Our experience is that sellers should seek to cash in on the majority of their business asset. If maintaining a minority stake, have a shareholder's agreement drawn up by an experienced lawyer.

Working for someone does not suit everybody, however with financial security achieved and the right attitude, it can be an interesting challenge. Okay, the new owner's decisions are not the ones you would make, but will they work? Better still, you can take a long weekend or holiday without worry about what is happening to the business.

The sale proceeds

"Some say the glass is half empty, some say the glass is half full, I say, are you going to drink that?"

Lisa Claymen

Traditionally owners' approach to sales proceeds has been that it must be enough to retire on or invest and maintain their 'current standard' of living. With luck and a very good business this remains achievable. Indeed, Avondale Group still help many clients achieve this goal. It is however getting harder because investment returns are much lower. In the nineties with a million you could have lived on say £80,000 a year. At the time of publishing it would probably generate c. £45,000 p.a. (maintaining the capital value), because of far lower interest and investment return rates.

Financial security need not however be the only goal. A sale might not be outright, or it could lead to a new career. You might at the time of sale pay the mortgage off or move to a cheaper area. Then again you might want or need a million or more for some special project that you have always dreamed of. You can now buy tourist tickets with NASA for example!

We find that people are happiest when they are working hard. The difference now is that the financial return need not be such a strong decider of what work you do. We believe the focus should be to work continuously on building wealth, but focus your energies on the type of wealth that you are poorest in.

Typically, many people tend to move to warmer climes for retirement – Europe, Spain and, to a lesser degree, Cyprus are common choices. America – Florida or California are others.

Our local abode may be where we have lived all of our lives. Our friends, relatives, children are all nearby and we are firmly rooted. On the other hand you could look at where you live in a different way. Your current place that you live could have been chosen more for economic than lifestyle reasons. If you live in a high cost belt, densely populated with high traffic congestion and pollution etc. it may be time to move. For your business you needed to be near the market that you supplied. There are many locations even around the UK where the property is less than half the price, the air ten times cleaner, the crime rate ten times lower.

A move could mean maintaining your living standard for half the monthly cost.

The sale proceeds (a summary)

1 Look in detail at all your financial assets and liabilities.
2 Forecast a reasonable and conservative estimate of your sale value in conjunction with a professional sale adviser.
3 Work out with your adviser your likely net proceeds after costs and tax.
4 Look carefully at how you intend to change your life in the next cycle.
5 Estimate your likely costs and income in your intended next cycle.
6 Work with a qualified financial adviser to consider how you will invest the proceeds and how this will enable you to live in the future.
7 Remember, if you have no liabilities, such as a mortgage, it is possible to live on less than you might need today running a business without a capital sum behind you.

Make sure your financial adviser is a specialist who also understands transactional business work and therefore is able to provide effective advice, in particular around the tax planning and investing the proceeds area. They should also have an insight into corporate financial planning so that your business needs can be considered. Select if you can an untied agent who can advise on a range of products and financial providers, not just one.

Retreat and think

"I never did a day's work in my life – it was all fun."

Thomas Edison

So you are, or will be, a successful owner/manager. Is now the right time to sell? In reality only you can answer that. Work of any sort can have many rewards apart from financial. By providing a useful service, we gain self-esteem, personal respect and value. To lose this without alternatives is dangerous. We suggest that, before you sell, or decide to sell, go on a retreat somewhere with your partner or by yourself. Think really deeply; think in a relaxed environment about your plan and your options.

Make a pros and cons list. Think about the things you want to do. Choose the probable next cycle.

A retreat can be a holiday but you should perhaps avoid too much non-stop touring, shopping and sightseeing. It should provide an opportunity to really relax and offer a period of time purely to yourself. Relaxation is the reduction of stimuli coming into the senses allowing the mind to clear out and get beneath day to day decisions and thoughts. How about a log cabin for peace, tranquillity, beauty and inspiration?

We think you should live as though you are going to live forever. Although we can learn and benefit from the past and plan and direct our future, in reality only the present exists today. So ask yourself: is what you are doing today, right now, deeply satisfying?

Enjoy!

CASE STUDY

SPECIALIST MAIL ORDER S.EAST
T/O £600,000, NP £145,000 — SOLD JANUARY 2003

Jim Smith is a man many of us would be envious of. Jim's hobby became his work and an important contribution to the community. Jim had joined the Army when he was 15 and developed a passion for electronics and communications, which was enhanced by specialist, high level work for the Army. After eleven years he left the Army and worked for a number of blue chip companies, developing new technology, before setting up his own company in 1975. His main work was as a sub-contractor for BAe but he also found time to develop and adapt electrical products for the blind, something he had been doing in his spare time for several years.

At first, 95% of the company's work came from BAe. However, after the Berlin Wall fell business dropped by 80% as BAe faced an uncertain future in the defence market. The company continued to carry out work for BAe but their main area of operation became the products for the disabled. They supplied tape recorders, low vision teaching equipment, dictaphones and loop systems to individuals, education authorities, universities and county councils. The majority of their clients were students who needed specialist equipment to continue their studies.

The business had the ethos that nothing was too much trouble and the staff was employed by their customers. As a result customer loyalty was very strong and long-established. Jim personally took great satisfaction from the service the company provided and the positive response he always had from his customers.

As he reached his sixties Jim had to make a decision about the future of the business and his involvement in it. Although he could have employed a general manager he would still have had to give personal assurances for all liabilities such as the lease, and he didn't want the ongoing responsibility hanging over him in his retirement. He therefore decided to sell the business.

Jim approached Kevin's (one of the authors) company Avondale Group who researched and brokered a sale for Jim. He received 70% of the consideration on day one with the rest deferred over two years. Jim's family still retain a small share in the company and Jim still pops in from time to time to lend a hand. The business has continued to expand and now turns over in excess of £1 million. The purchaser, who already owned a number of niche mail order interests, is now adding to his group of companies.

As for Jim, since his retirement he has travelled the world, taking in the sights of Australia, New Zealand and America, and celebrated his silver wedding anniversary in style on a yacht.

chapter four What is it worth? – The professional's viewpoint

FOUR What is it worth? – The professional's viewpoint

"Honest disagreement is often a good sign of progress."

Mahatma Gandhi

"Markets are constantly in a state of uncertainty and flux and money is made by discounting the obvious and betting on the unexpected."

George Soros

Chapter focus

To explain how small to medium-sized businesses are valued in straightforward yet comprehensive terms.

- **Introduction**
- **The formula**
- **The multiple**
- **What multiple?**
- **What profit?**
- **Sale structure**
- **Asset and goodwill deals versus share transfers**
- **Revaluing the balance sheet (share transfers)**
- **The optimum purchaser, the optimum valuation**
- **Should I be selling?**
- **Art not science**
- **The valuation steps (a summary)**

Introduction

Valuations of businesses are a matter of opinion. A business is worth as much as a buyer is prepared to pay for it and as much as a seller is prepared to sell for. A valuation will normally seek to measure the trust a market has in a business and in its ability to create wealth (the goodwill). A professional valuation should establish the fair market value a willing and informed buyer would purchase a company for in normal open market conditions. Goodwill is intangible, although the accounting definition is the difference between the purchase price and the company's balance sheet assets (net assets).

The formula

There are many different techniques for calculating the value of a business. Typically in unquoted smaller businesses the most usual method is to use a multiple of one year's maintainable profits. The chosen multiple is the number of years it is considered acceptable to generate a payback on the investment. This can be expressed as a formula:

Multiple x Maintainable Profit per annum pre tax (pa)
= Likely Valuation

Or to work the equation backwards if you know the price paid

Price paid/Maintainable Profit pre tax (pa).
= Price Earnings ratio (number of years to generate payback)

Or if you know the price paid/agreed and you want to work out the return on capital employed (normally used to compare return against other possible investments)

Net maintainable profit pre tax (pa)/price paid x 100 = % Return on capital employed (ROCE)

The multiple

A multiple for smaller private businesses is based on its desirability dependent upon market forces, perceived risk and buyer's individual circumstances. The higher the multiple the more desirable and sustainable the business is thought to be. This means the acceptable payback period is longer, or the acceptable earnings per share/equity are lower. Individual circumstances can have a significant effect. A buyer offering a linked product with cross-selling opportunities, client synergy and the ability to benefit from economies of scale is likely to attach a higher multiple to a business than a buyer that reaps no obvious direct benefits. Multiples are also dictated in comparison to the return other investments can make.

How do the markets perceive an appropriate multiple for a business? The following list is not exhaustive, nor in any particular order. It provides some examples of the aspects that should be taken into consideration when choosing a multiple.

1 Industry sector

2 Assumed level of profits

3 Business size

4 Quality and sustainability of earnings

5 Track record of growth

6 The strength and true value of the asset base/debt levels

7 Growing market trend/demographics

8 Cost of expansion (high or low investment required to create growth)

9 Location, pleasant business environment

10 Brand strength

11 Customer loyalty (strength of contracts if any)

12 Strength and reliability of cash flow

13 Ability to finance

14 Research and development

15 Intellectual property (patents, ideas, copyrights, research and development)

16 Deal structure (an 'earn out' deal is lower risk and may drive a higher multiple.)

17 People, desirability of (skilled staff and management)

18 Fad (the 'in thing')

19 Market comparison (listed companies, quoted current value and other SME deals recently done)

20 The level of contingent (possible) liabilities in the future (share transfers)

21 The level of risk in a business.

What multiple?

Methods used to value businesses include industry specific formulas, asset-based valuations, discount cashflow forecasts (DCF) and dividend formulas. However, a multiple calculation is by far the most common method used.

In recent years smaller business multiples have run from as low as 1 to as strong as 14 times (post-tax) net profit earnings. The high multiples quoted here only relate to the largest businesses within the small to medium-sized (SME) sector and include private companies converting to public status (flotation's). This reflects the strength of their earnings and in the case of floated businesses, the availability of their shares to the public providing an accessible ongoing trading market. In general terms, as private companies get larger with higher profits and more infrastructure they are worth more. This is because larger businesses usually offer:

- More economies of scale enhancing a potential buyer's likely profit.
- A better infrastructure, systems, management and asset base.
- A higher quality and sustainability of earnings.
- A wider appeal to global buyers with deeper, more accessible pockets.
- A strong brand, established customers and goodwill behind their profits.

The average multiple in the SME market is, at the time of writing, in the low to mid range of these figures, e.g. 2 – 8 (post-tax). Of the factors given previously, it is usually the size of a business, level of profit, asset base, sector and market conditions that are the most significant factors involved when choosing a multiple.

Size

Whilst there are some 3.8 million business in the UK, most of these are one-man operations or quasi-jobs and therefore very difficult to sell. In 2001 DTI statistics estimate that there are some 600,000 UK employers earning in excess of £75,000 net profit.

Asset base

Multiples are principally about the treatment of goodwill; the intangible asset reflected ultimately by how much profit a business makes. But what about the tangibles, such as the fixtures, equipment, plant, freehold or the stock? Depending on the size of a deal, the tangibles are usually accounted for in part in the total multiple applied for the goodwill. This may sound harsh but, ultimately, there is in general no point to business assets unless they generate a return, thus the multiple should take into consideration these assets. However, some adjustments can be made to the multiple, for companies with highly saleable fixed assets such as a freehold, desirable plant or vehicles. A common adjustment with freeholds is to strip them out of the equation altogether, to value the business on a leasehold basis after accounting for rent. Cash assets over and above the working capital requirements of the business are also usually stripped out before a sale.

Intellectual property (IP) has a value. It is very difficult to determine. For most established businesses the IP or R&D (research and development) will already reflect in the profits of a business and therefore multiplying the profits will value the IP. In some key cases, this may not be true. Some products, typically software or medical for example, have a knowledge that has far greater potential than the current profits generated. Where this is the case the potential should be assessed and estimated and perhaps a cash flow forecast valuation carried out against this potential. Alternatively, enhancing the multiple may also apply.

Sector

Different sectors command different multiples reflecting the market's perception of a specific sector. Perception normally reflects demographic, environmental, social, competitive and economic trends. It is also usually dictated by the expected lifecycle of a product, the size of its market, expandability and level of risk. Strong sectors are generally expanding, well perceived and sustainable. Businesses in the sector will generally have a low cost of expansion and enjoy good trading conditions and prospects. Occasionally a sector's perception can be influenced by fashion or 'fads'.

Market conditions

Multiples will also be dictated by market conditions. In general SME businesses have robust multiples whatever the economic conditions. Acquisitions can be attractive alternatives to organic growth. Indeed, in some highly competitive sectors organic growth (internal investment) bears little fruit, making acquisition the only option to increase market share whilst maintaining margin. Even in an economic slowdown many buyers struggle for margin and, by combining two operations, economies of scale can be reaped (1 plus 1 = 3, otherwise known as synergy). If interest rates are low the purchase may be financed cheaply.

Probable SME factor range

Low multiple	High multiple
Less desirable SME business	Desirable SME business
Poor expansion	Highly expandable
Declining sector (poorly perceived)	Growth sector (well perceived)

Multiple	2	3	4	5	6	7	8
Net profit	£75,000	£75,000	£200,000 0	£300,000	£500,000	£500,000	£500,000
Possible goodwill	£150,000 0	£225,000 0	£800,000 0	£1,500,000 0	£3,000,000 0	£3500,000 0	4,000000 0

The above assumes that:

- A UK company; sterling.
- The sale is a share transfer
- That the net assets have been rationalized to the material trading needs of the business (enterprise value) and therefore are included in the goodwill.
- That the balance sheet shows all assets at its true open market resale value and all liabilities are identified, i.e. that there are no adverse contingent (possible) liabilities that affect the value.

What profit?

An acquirer is buying the ability to create future profit, but what is the underlying level of true profit? The historic net profit has been spent. The accounts may be unaudited and were probably produced for the Inland Revenue. One person's costs may be different to another. What can we do?

The net profit used for a valuation is usually based on last year's maintainable net profit. This is the profit a buyer is likely to maintain after taking account of the seller's personal and extraordinary costs. Questions will need to be asked and assumptions made. These might include:

- What is the quality of the earnings?
- Is an average of past profit realistic or is last year's profit more reflective of future earnings?
- Has the profit historically been reliable at this level?
- Is the cost base sustainable?
- Are there any one-off costs likely to be incurred in the future?
- What is next year's realistic forecast?
- Are the forecasts realistic and how expandable is the business?
- Will the customers stay with the business?
- Is the market or business expanding or contracting?
- Will the contracts continue?
- Is the market evolving?
- Are there any environmental, demographic or social trends likely to affect future earnings?
- Is the business competitive and likely to remain competitive?
- Are the customers high or low risk?

A sustainable profit figure will be assumed, often using last year's net profit as a base. It is then normal to make specific adjustments to this figure to obtain the net profit to a buyer, rather than the one the previous owner may have enjoyed. This is called calculating the adjusted net profit. The below list is by no means exhaustive but shows the sort of adjustments that might be made.

Adjustments to the net profit might include 'add backs' such as the seller's:

- salary, or
- extraordinary or personal costs.

Adjustments to the net profit might include 'add ons' such as:

- Costs for placing the business under management.
- Additional premises cost if requiring relocation.
- Investment required replacing old equipment.

Typically, in smaller private companies the adjusted net profit will be calculated:

- Using the last full financial year's profit figure.
- On a 'stand alone' basis, without the economies of scale or synergies, that a buyer may bring, being taken into account.
- Under management basis, rather than a working owner.
- Post-tax.

Sale structure

A valuation will also be affected by the sale structure. Before valuing a business it is important to ascertain what is and isn't included and its legal entity. With a limited company it is normal to sell the shares of a business (a share transfer). This means the buyer assumes all the liabilities (both known and unknown!) and assets in the company. Any deal will therefore include the net asset value of the company, being the balance sheet reserve of a company. This will alter through normal trading fluctuations, for example profit may be left in as cash, building up the net asset value (shareholders' funds).

Sole traders and partners are usually sold on a fixed asset and goodwill basis (a goodwill and asset sale), which means that the seller will retain, to collect in and pay off the debtors and creditors. Typically the seller will keep their bank account, leaving the buyer to stump up working capital. Most buyers will account for working capital requirements by reducing the goodwill they are paying by the level of working capital, so they get an overall multiple.

With share transfers most buyers will tend to only want to buy the net asset at enterprise value, that is the lowest that is required for normal trading levels in the company. This means sellers may be required to take a pre-sale dividend for example, or sell off a freehold prior to sale.

Buyers will also seek to only pay the true resale value of assets, not the book value. The book value will be there for historic accounting purposes, including tax planning or aggressive depreciation policies. For example, it is not uncommon to find freeholds undervalued in the balance sheet (the books) or vehicles over valued on their open market resale value. Both these items have an intrinsic value away from the business and do not need a trading entity to sell. Stock can be harder to value, as in some businesses its purchase value at cost would not be realizable if in worst case the business went bust. Where are you going to sell it – a car boot? Stock therefore is often down-valued by buyers on purchase. For purchasers, ascertaining the true value of the assets being brought in a Limited Company is a significant part of the due diligence (checking) process prior to completing an acquisition. Not to mention trying to assess any contingent liabilities (potential liabilities) that the balance sheet does not show, but which the buyer may inherit with the shares they buy.

Whatever the sale structure the valuation technique is the same, although the type of sale, whether assets or shares, will have a bearing on the assets and liabilities being included in the deal and will therefore have a bearing on the multiple chosen.

Asset and goodwill deals versus share transfers

With a Limited Company it is possible, rather than carrying out a share transfer for a sale, for the company to become the vendor and to sell its name, assets and goodwill. In this case the money is transferred into the company, the shareholders then liquidate the business to get at the proceeds. By acquiring a business this way the purchaser avoids taking over any contingent liabilities that might come with the shares. They can also amortize the goodwill over time, which means they can offset the purchase against future profits to save tax.

Whilst this works in theory, there are two problems: firstly, that the seller incurs a double tax charge which most sellers will want to avoid at all costs. Secondly, that many contracts that have been given to a Limited

Company may not be easily transferable to a new entity, e.g. leases or approved supplier status.

If shares are transferred staff automatically get continuous employment, as there is no change of employer. Currently, for asset and goodwill deals the 'transfer of undertakings for protection of employment' (TUPE) legislation stands. This means staff are automatically transferred on their existing conditions to the new employer at the time of transfer and they achieve continuous employment and all the rights that entails.

In the UK (where we are based) under the current tax regime, assuming contracts are transferable, most buyers will prefer to buy assets and goodwill rather than shares. Sellers will prefer to sell shares to avoid a potential double tax charge. Usually sellers win because even buyers can see that sellers will not tolerate a double tax charge. Both parties should refer to their professional advisers as early as possible in the deal-making process before making any assumptions.

Asset sales	Advantages	Disadvantages
Buyers	Can amortize goodwill, reducing profits saving tax Creates a clean purchase avoiding hidden or contingent liabilities (skeletons in the cupboard) Less due diligence and faster completion Lower professional fees	Contracts may not transfer easily Transfer of undertakings and protection of employment (TUPE) legislation can be difficult for buyers seeking to change staff contracts for integration reasons after purchase Any leases will need 'assigning' which is time consuming
Sellers	Less legal costs or onerous contracts due to clean break Less due diligence and faster completion Can rollover the proceeds to offset double tax charge (??)	Sellers can face a double tax charge, as the company is the vendor; it pays corporation tax on profit on sale of goodwill. Then the sellers pay more tax when taking the proceeds out of the company

Revaluing the balance sheet (share transfers)

Whilst it is true buyers look mainly at the overall return on capital employed, when they buy shares (companies) they will also look at the reserve of the balance sheet should things go wrong. The less they pay for goodwill and the more they pay for realizable reserve should they need to liquidate at a later date, the lower the risk of the venture. This means that:

- They may accept a lower return on capital on the amount of money they pay against a balance sheet.
- They should accept that the closer the reserve is to the price the more up front they should pay (less performance-related).

A balance sheet is a historic snapshot of a company reserves. In theory it is what the business would have if it ceased trading on that day once it has collected everything it is owed and paid off everything it owes. Unfortunately, balance sheets are however subjective. They are based on accounting policies, which may not be accurate. Therefore, to value companies you need to calculate the true net asset value of a business.

To calculate the 'true net asset value' go through every item line by line on the balance sheet. Is everything worth what it should be? For example:

- Does the company over depreciate or under depreciate fixed assets? What is the true resale value of the assets on the open market given the type of equipment it is and the time that might be allowed to seller (fast means cheap)?
- Has the property in a company appreciated?
- Is the stock really realizable at that value, particularly if the business were closed? Where would you sell it, at a car boot?
- Is the stock perishable or last season's?
- Is there goodwill or research and development capitalized in the balance sheet, which we will be re-selling elsewhere? These need to be taken out of a balance sheet if you want to find the true reserve value.
- Will all trade debtors be collectable?
- Are all creditors required to be paid off?

- Directors' loans (repayment is potentially a payment for goodwill, as these are often a means of putting equity in a business, if it cannot finance itself in other ways).
- Should and will a pre-sale dividend need to be taken to reduce the cash at bank? Buyers don't generally want surplus cash in the deal.

The optimum purchaser, the optimum valuation

In order to value a business and to obtain the best price it is essential to have in mind the likely buyer. Better still, several buyers in order to obtain competitive market appeal. The optimal purchaser is one who has a 'we want, we need' motivation:

- Who are willing to pay a premium
- Can add value by synergy or economies/management
- Has vision for the business
- Does not have regulatory/monopoly constraints
- Has the funds and the strategy today
- Understands the business and has the people to run it
- Is sensible about their 'investigations' into the business (due diligence) and the sale contract they will require

So who will pay the most and what motivates each type of buyer?

Acquirer type	Positive	Negative
Direct competitors	Understands your value Will benefit from economies of scale Will have management to run it May need to buy to maintain growth as organic growth is slow Funding usually accessible	Confidentiality May be 'researching' rather than buying Requires board approval and strategies change leaving risk of a last minute reversal
Companies in related industries	Values 'know how' especially if they don't have it. Could enjoy economies of scale (cost savings) Could enjoy synergies (cross-selling for example) Should have management to run it Funding usually accessible	May be 'researching' rather than buying Requires board approval and strategies change Risk of last minute reversal
Suppliers/ customers	As above	May damage your goodwill if the process goes wrong
Overseas buyer	Wants foothold in your country	Does not have cultural understanding
MBI/MBO (Management buy in/buy out)	No research finding process Understand the business more Management's track-record can help funding	Existing management may end up damaging business if MBO fails Pay less as leveraging the cash Entirely subject to the financier's decision
Financial purchasers (Private equity houses/venture capitalists)	Will look at all types of trade Can leave vendors significant stake	No synergies Looking for low risk Don't understand the trade
Individuals	Can act quickly (no board strategy/ politics to consider) Take risks	Will buy for the enjoyment of the job/business rather than just the financial return Investing their savings or borrowing so can be conservative and unreliable/whimsical Pockets are usually not deep No economies or synergy

Should I be selling?

Many professionals will say a business is worth what someone will pay for it. This is true, but it is also worth what someone will sell it for. A business may be worth more to the seller than to the buyer. Most valuations are carried out assuming a sale has been decided upon and that there is a reason to sell it. In other words, assuming there is a willing seller. However, our experience is that the motivations and willingness of sellers vary and this does have a bearing on the value to them. For many sellers, their business is often their largest asset and only income source.

As a seller, prior to accepting a sale, it is vital to consider in detail your objectives. It is important with your own strategic position in mind to have a clear bottom line. If you are an owner/manager you need also to consider your personal, financial and lifestyle position. Your bottom line is where it is worth selling versus keeping the business. This bottom line should be based on the net proceeds, which is the total sale price less tax and less professional costs. In the case of an owner/manager the decision to sell might balance the following:

Likely net proceeds

Versus

Current personal financial position	Personal motivation/ strategy	Business strategy
• Will the mortgage be paid off? • If so can I live on less? • What are investment yields? • Am I relocating and is the cost of living cheaper or higher there? • Will I continue working? • Have I a pension?	• Am I retiring? • What will I do next? • Am I opting for a different lifestyle? • How is my health? • What do the family need/want? • Do I like what I do?	• Can I continue to expand? • Have I the right team? • Do I need to invest heavily to grow? • What is the market trend? • What is the competition doing? • Do I need 2nd tier management?

Tax

Depending in which tax environment (country/region) your business is sold, tax on any capital gain you make will probably be your biggest cost. The rule here is to get professional advice early on in order to secure the most profitable sale. Currently in the UK (where we reside) 'taper relief', an Inland Revenue allowance, makes selling an attractive option. Taper relief reduces a chargeable gain according to how long you held the asset before you disposed of it. The relief is given after all other reliefs and allowances. The amount of the reduction depends on how long you held the asset (the qualifying holding period) and whether the asset was a business asset or a non-business asset. Taper relief creates a significant argument for entrepreneurs to make money through capital gain rather than through ongoing profits.

UK – Taper relief on business assets on or after 6th April 2002	
Number of whole years in the qualifying holding period. This is from the date on which you acquired the asset, or 6th April 1998	Gain remaining chargeable %
Less than 1	100
1	50
2 or more	25

Based on tax rates at the time of writing the above could mean paying only 10% tax on any capital gain made, but please refer to your professional tax advisor before making an assumption as taper relief is not always as straightforward as it first seems. In order to protect your sale proceeds for your family in the future it is also sensible to take advice regarding your inheritance tax position.

Costs

Sellers also need to allow for professional costs including a merger and acquisition advisor, a tax advisor and a lawyer. These costs vary but you get what you pay for. For smaller companies professional costs are usually between 5-10% of the proceeds. Some of the costs will be prior to the sale. This will also vary depending on currency.

Net proceeds

Small companies usually generate a good investment return and the decision to sell can therefore be difficult. One way to help is to compare the likely income they will achieve after tax if they continue running the business versus the net sale proceeds. They should then factor in the power of an assured capital sum (pay off borrowings or provide investment income) versus potential future earnings after income tax and any future earnings potential they may still have in the future, if the seller intends to continue working in some capacity. Ultimately all the number crunching in the world will not make the decision, it will just clarify the facts. The decision must also be made in context to the lifestyle reasons of the owner/manager and the strategic position of the business.

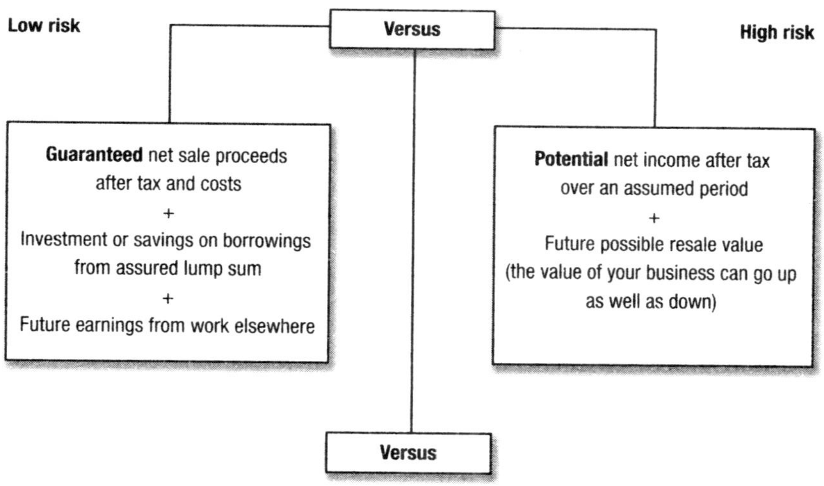

Art not science

The adjustments that are reasonable and acceptable to make to the net profit are a matter of opinion. The multiple or length of time acceptable for pay back is also a matter of opinion. They depend on the buying and selling parties' point of view. Also what assets are necessary? Should they all be included in the sale, and on an open market what is their resale value compared to a distress situation? No two organizations or individuals are the same and therefore opinions will differ.

Consequently, valuations are an art not a science. Knowing the formula to value a company is not enough. Having an instinct and a comparison (past experience) is also vital. Knowing the market and the way the likely buyer will operate is essential. Only an organization or someone that is constantly completing deals can therefore hope to give a near accurate forecast of valuation. Even then, a true professional will always admit that their valuation is a forecast of what the market will assume and that markets are notoriously fickle both upwards and downwards. It is also important to remember that a valuation is an estimate at a given point of time. Profits change and so do market conditions, perceptions and assumptions.

Good negotiators buy cheaper businesses and sell more expensive ones; it's that simple. So if you are buying or selling it is also important to understand how to negotiate, as well as how to value a business. Timing also plays a crucial part... buy near the bottom and sell near the peak. If you know when that is, please call us!

The valuation steps (a summary)

1. Guess or estimate who your buyer/seller will be.
2. Calculate an adjusted sustainable net profit that buyer/seller is likely to make.
3. Be reasonable and conservative on adjustments to the profits.
4. Normally, work on a business under management (staff run) basis.
5. Rationalize/review assets. Work out what will be included in a sale and likely sale structure. Will it be a share transfer or an asset deal? Is there intellectual property?
6. If buying assets, what is their true resale value? How does this affect the multiple?
7. Talk to an experienced active dealmaker who understands the sector to obtain a multiple appropriate for the size and type of business.
8. Multiple x Adjusted Profit per annum (pa) = Likely Valuation
9. Check the final Return on capital employed. If you spend £1 will you get back profits in a year of 10p, 20p, 25p, or 50p? If it's 20p it's a five-year pay back pre-finance/tax.

10 Ask yourself would you pay this, in comparison to other investments?

11 If you are acquiring, balance your return on capital employed to strategic need to buy.

12 If you are selling, balance your final net proceeds (after tax and costs) to willingness/strategic reason to sell.

The value of a private business is the price achieved by a willing seller and willing buyer for the controlling interest on the day of completion.

chapter five A buyer's guide – The good, the bad and the ugly

FIVE A buyer's guide – The good, the bad and the ugly

"You only have to do a very few things right in your life so long as you don't do too many things wrong."

Warren Buffett

"Flaming enthusiasm, backed by horse sense and persistence, is the quality that most frequently makes for success."

Dale Carnegie

Chapter focus

What to look for when considering a business purchase, and also what to be wary of.

- **Introduction**
- **Getting started**
- **Timing the purchase**
- **Researching and setting your strategy**
- **Sources of businesses**
- **Handling the seller**
- **Look for potential**
- **Staff meeting**
- **Due diligence checklist**
- **Potential purchase timetable**

Introduction

If you already own a business and are thinking of selling you may wish to skip this chapter, although it is useful when selling to get insights into the buyer's strategy and requirements. Buying a business successfully requires effective planning, knowledge and a clear strategy. In this chapter we focus on the practical aspects of the process. We have assumed that you have some strategy over what to buy, and why you are focusing on a particular sector, so we only briefly touch on this subject. If you don't have a strategy of what to buy, setting one is a vital first step.

In this chapter our aim is to save you time by getting you started. Buying is a complex process and this chapter is not definitive. Professional advice should be taken. Negotiation is a specialist subject, whether buying or selling, and has it's own chapter later. Understanding the financing process prior to starting your search for a purchase is essential to appreciate how much you can afford and how potentially to structure the deal. We cover this in the next chapter, as fund raising can form an important component of business planning. It is of course not possible to exactly identify how to finance a deal until a purchase is found as there are many variables including how much funds can be raised against the assets of the business.

Getting started

Buying and searching can take up a lot of time if you let it. One way to shorten the process is through preparation. We suggest the following steps before you undertake the project.

- Line up good professional advisors from the start (see Chapter 10 for ideas on choosing an intermediary).
- Understand and research the purchase process continuously
- Be aware of your funding options
- Analyze and be clear on why and what you are going to buy
- Be clear on your objectives and strategy
- Set out realistic criteria and stick to it
- Research target sector in depth (market trends, competitors, legalization, threats, opportunities, demographics)

- Dedicate time to the process
- Draw up a timetable and action plan.

Timing the purchase

When to buy? Buy when the market is low, and sell when the market is high. It's obvious but difficult to forecast. In reality the only way to predict is via analysis of information, research and instinct. Look at economic data, past trends and use common sense. Many people will buy a company's shares during a boom when the industry they are looking at is doing well. Consequently the price can be high. The trick is to predict the boom, or buy mid-cycle, not at the top. When there are boom conditions many average companies can ride on the crest of the wave, have good profits and growth.

The IT recruitment industry during the late 90s and early 2000s was textbook boom and bust, with many investors coming in late on the boom. At one time even graduates with inexperience were achieving average salaries of over £80,000 per year in this high margin industry. Could that last? One year later, with the turndown in the requirement for highly paid IT staff, this value did not just drop it disappeared. Six vacancies chasing every IT contractor turned to six contractors chasing every vacancy. Many companies went into liquidation, profits turned to loss, and companies became half the size that they previously were. All in the space of a few months. Valuations based on profit multiples went from £multi-millions to zero over the period of one quarter.

The point we are making is that when you buy a company you are buying the future profits, not the current ones. Past profits are only an indicator of the future profits trend. The true figure you need to calculate is what you expect the profits to be. This means you make your mind up on future performance, and don't just follow the crowd.

Markets are notoriously difficult to predict and even the experts get it wrong. It is sometimes better and simpler to buy when it is right for you, and rely on a good purchase strategy and strong business plan for your purchase. This will always enable you to buy at the right time (cheap), because you will be able to build on the base that the purchase has provided. Valuations based on a multiple of profits, reflecting how the company was historically run, is the market norm, and this can produce companies on offer at below their real value and potential. If well run (by you), it is the people, product and idea that really dictate a business's future vaiue. Finding and targeting an acquisition of a company that is doing well, regardless of market conditions, and that has potential can be the most effective route to buying at the right time.

Researching and setting your strategy

A good purchase strategy is subjective, and it is only with hindsight that you will tell if the plan worked. Many of the reasons businesses are valued higher (see Chapter 4) is because the business offers strong reasons for purchase; however, how can you look at your position and set your strategy? We suggest the following be considered as a start:

- Assess your targets for cultural alignment with your personal values, or existing organization's approach.
- Look for potential, market growth and expansion prospects.
- Identify strong future economic demographics in your chosen sector.
- Decide if you are an existing company seeking economies of scale and cross-synergies.
- Be realistic about your ability to change the target.
- Avoid arrogance.
- Listen to others but determine your own mind. A bad purchase decision implemented with conviction is often better than a good decision implemented tentatively.

Research is also essential. Do your own quick competitor analysis by ringing companies as a customer and record their responses. Here are ten suggested questions to assess each. You may like to change these reflecting the particular type of industry.

- How many rings to answer the phone?
- Was the voice on answering the phone polite, helpful and positive-sounding?
- Was I put through efficiently to the right person?
- Did they have any special offers or promotions?

- Can you (in the proposed business purchase) offer something better than them?
- Do they have something to offer that you cannot?
- Did they ask for your name and number?
- What are their prices like?
- Do they have a clear market niche?
- How many marks out of ten would you give their response to you?

One of us recently bumped into a friend loitering in a local town on a Saturday morning. It turned out he and his wife were researching. They were looking at retail establishments with a view to setting up a niche estate agency for overseas properties. Walk down the high street at different times, notice the traffic. Go in to the businesses as a customer. Talk to other people that are shopping. Send friends out to meet the sales representatives under false pretences. Research, research and more research.

The friends found out that demand for services was very high but customers were very dissatisfied and untrusting of the people they were dealing with; hard, pushy sales people seriously put people off making an enquiry in the first place. The opportunity was clearly in offering a service in a radically different way providing a consultative selling approach.

Industry associations and trade bodies will all provide you with information on their sectors, usually for free on their website. They will also probably have a magazine you can subscribe to. Read up on the industry, find out the trends. Is the industry likely to grow? Or is the industry running outdated practices that are waiting to be updated? There will also be businesses for sale in such publications. You can also attend trade shows and exhibitions, most are free. A day so invested can give you a tremendous amount of knowledge and contacts.

The Internet is a great research tool. You can even obtain target companies or competitors' accounts via the Internet so long as they are companies (not sole traders-partnerships).

Sources of businesses

There are many ways to find a business for acquisition. There is an old saying that everything is for sale at the right price, so identifying and targeting possible acquisitions by direct approaches to non-active vendors is one way. The other and probably easier way is via sources of vendors who are actively seeking a sale. The active vendors are probably easier as generally they have a thought-through motive for sale and are likely therefore to be both more realistic and prepared, particularly if they have employed a good broker. The advantage of the direct approach is it can avoid competition with other buyers and can be a good second phase if there are no active vendor targets that suit your criteria, however be wary of greedy and unprepared sellers. There are many. We have listed below many sources along with some of the pros and cons of each. When you contact your advisors be positive and take time to explain your requirements preferably via a pre-prepared brief.

Source of Businesses	Pros	Cons
Sale Brokers	Professionally valued Prepared and realistic vendor (usually) Professional advice Middleman in negotiations No fee to you If you tell them what you are looking for they will keep you in mind Prepared sale information Saves time	Broker represents seller Good brokers create competitive process and find more than one buyer to push price up
Acquisition Brokers	Saves your time Offers a buffer to direct targeted approach for vendors increasing their likelihood of opening discussions increasing audience of vendors Cost usually offset by broadening audience of potential businesses	Upfront expense (usually)
Personal Contacts	Might know the business itself and have a trusting relationship with the seller	

Source of Businesses	Pros	Cons
Speculative Enquiries	Might dig up good opportunity that no one else knows about	Time consuming Unrealistic perception of value in vendor's eyes Unprepared vendors without prepared information
Auctions	Prices can be attractive	Must do all due diligence and valuation before attending auction
For Sale By Owner	Unlikely to find as many interested buyers Inexperienced vendors offer potential to chip away at price Naïve vendors can under-value	Needs research to track down willing sellers Unrealistic perception of value in vendor's eyes Uncertain seller lacking in appropriate professional advice

Sources of Direct sellers/Brokers	
National Press & web	Daltons, Financial Times, Sunday Times, Financial Mail, Evening Standard
Internet:	www.Businessesforsale.com www.Buybiz.com www.business-sale.com www.Daltonbusiness.com www.avondale.co.uk www.loot.com www.bizsale.co.uk www.nationwidebusiness.co.uk www.startupinbusiness.co.uk www. startups.co.uk
Research	Databases such as FAME, Dunn and Bradstreet
Recommendations	Recommendations: Banks, Accountants, Lawyers, Business Links
Trade press	Per sector. See **http://www.intellagencia.com** for trade publication lists
Advice	Advice: www.businesslink.gov.uk

Handling the seller

Many buyers see their approach to the seller as adversarial. That is, they see the buying process as one where they have to win. This is very dangerous particularly with the purchase of historically owner-managed businesses. The goodwill may rely on the outgoing party more heavily than you realize and the buyer more often or not will need to rely on the seller's goodwill after purchase.

Find out quickly what is driving the seller. The ideal seller is a motivated one. Make sure they are driven by personal circumstances, not something bad about to happen to their business. Why do they really want to sell? Are they telling you the truth, the whole truth and nothing but the truth? What will they really sell for? How influential is their partner on them? How key is their role really? Is there anything that they don't want you to find out? Are they serious about selling or are they just testing the market? What does their body language tell you? What are their expectations after sale?

This is a two way process. You will need to get the most out of the seller to reveal your motivations and situation. Often, particularly if being handled by a broker, you may need to provide evidence of your financial ability and to provide an undertaking to ensure that the information given to you on the target is confidential.

If it is an owner/manager selling it is highly likely that they will have an emotional connection to the enterprise. Be aware and respect this, it may well work in your favour, particularly if you play on sentiment to get the price down. Reassuring the seller that you care about the future of the seller's business as much as they do will give comfort to uncertain sellers. Try yourself to avoid emotion, maintaining an objective overview of your discussions, yet at the same time present enthusiasm to the seller about what you offer.

What a seller wants for a business should not really influence you that much. Do your own calculation of its value to you, irrespective, and then close a deal at this figure or below, or walk. If you find a business you like, but not at a price you like, make a firm offer anyway. Every month send the seller a reminder that your offer still stands. There is nothing like time with nothing new coming up to reduce the price in the seller's mind. Patience is a virtue few entrepreneurs have because they have learnt to deal with things urgently to survive and beat the competition.

If the seller is not getting exactly what they've asked for, they want to sit around for a while and find out what other offers are going to be made. When the offers stop, their mood changes. If they are sitting around and feeling disheartened because nobody has given them a realistic offer, and you've been consistently interested, they might just call you. Keep looking until the ideal conditions are met.

Prepare the questions you want to ask and the answers you can expect to be asked by the seller. In summary these should include preparation for the following in addition to any relating to the specific enterprise in question.

Look for potential

In 2000 Philip Green brought the UK based High Street retailer BHS with over 160 stores for £220 million. After just two years BHS reported a 202% profit increase. Analysts valued the business at over 6 times its purchase price; some improvement. Green brought a poorly perceived business, which was considered by many to have had its day, then with tight financial controls changed the way the business thought about itself, in particular in the buying area. They were very tough on suppliers driving purchase down. Just think: 1- 2% extra margin on sales of Y = an increase in profits on the bottom line of X, less any cost involved in negotiating.

When you look at a business and assess its value, you are assessing your own or your organization's ability to take it forward. You are after all buying its future profits, not its historic profits. So you need to know what resources you have that can add value to a business. These can include financial muscle, knowledge and contacts within an industry, sales or marketing expertise, or just a very creative commercial mind that can see opportunities that others miss.

You do not want to buy an average business with limited potential at a bargain price. You do not even want to buy an excellent business with limited potential at a bargain price. The potential is the key. If the current business owns a corner shop and is keeping it open virtually all hours, then there is probably little scope for development.

The potential can sometimes be found by looking at it a different way, and it works just as well on a smaller scale than BHS. A friend, Homayoon Fassihi, bought a small laundrette some time ago in Norwich with a flat above. The laundrette was really at potential in terms of local residents. However, the 12 machines were inoperative for about 15 of the 24 hour day. The marginal cost of running a machine was next to nothing. So Homayoon walked into hairdressers in Norwich and said to the owners, "You obviously need to wash a lot of towels every day, how much does it cost you?" The answer was that they sent one of the staff to a local laundrette and paid the slot price. Homayoon said, "I will pick them up and deliver them back to you at any time you like for less price than you are paying now, plus you have your staff back instead of sitting in a laundrette. Can I have the business please?" He expanded to other hairdressers, theatres, government instructions and even airlines. Soon his machines were working 23 out of 24 hours. Clearly at this point growth was limited and he moved on. Talk about a money making machine!

Business owners can get so focused on day-to-day management issues that by definition they rarely get the chance to stand back and look at the bigger picture objectively. Thinking big and objectively can mean that you can see different routes to exploit for profit that have been missed. A company for example, might be selling most of its wares via its web pages. Yet have they explored the idea of selling via other people's web pages on a sales commission basis? This is an example of an idea asset. No financial resource is required here and yet the idea alone, when put into action, can make a big difference. Whatever a company sells, there will always be alternative routes to market. Uncover one and you can buy yourself a bargain and be in for a capital gain in a relatively short period of time.

As well as growth opportunities, most businesses offer cost savings. We all understand the difference between a profit and a loss. What fewer understand is the concept of a hidden loss. A hidden loss is the difference between the profits made and the profits that could or even should have been made. Buying a business is not just about analyzing the profits and losses but looking for the hidden losses. Are there too many staff, could better systems speed up production, etc.

The following is a list of some of the things we look for in an acquisition. Clearly each purchaser will have his or her own requirements. We use a very basic grading system to score each target. It does not matter what the technique is so long as the scores are kept objective, impartial and consistent across each potential target. We use 10 as good.

A. Basic grading model		
B. The good	**C. Grade 1-10**	**D. The bad and the ugly**
Motivated seller		The opposite is usually in the bad and ugly, but be wary of grading bad as a downside. Some bad elements in a business present opportunity. Look for negatives that can be turned around but also used as a bargaining chip.
Strong retainable management workforces		
Strong matching culture		
Strategic match with ideas		
Sustainable profit record		
Economies of scale obtainable		
Clear and unique brand		
Location or market limits potential		
Quality personnel		
Cost savings		
Strong track record		
Low cost of expansion		
Expandability		
Strong on-going customer relationships/contracts		
Affordability		
What barriers to entry are there		
Strong systems		

Build your business plan before completing the acquisition. There are arguments to say don't implement it until you have had the opportunity to listen and really get a feel for the business. However, much of what you are buying is, we hope, the potential for growth, so having some ideas on how these can be achieved is a pre-requisite prior to every acquisition. Ask:

Staff:

- What motivates you?
- What ideas for improvement do you have?
- What training would be appropriate to improve productivity?
- What decision could be made right now, to make your job easier?

Customers:

- Who shall I meet with first?
- Can we offer anything extra to them?
- Why do our current customers use us?
- Can/should our prices be raised?

Operations:

- What is the least efficient process in the company?
- How effective are the IT systems?

Marketing:

- Have they got an effective web presence?
- What advantage do they have over our competitors?
- What opportunity are they under-exploiting?
- Have they a clear market niche?
- Are they focused?
- Should they move away from certain types of customer?
- What free advertising resources can we take advantage of?
- Are there any synergistic partnerships we could make?

Finance:

- How can cash flow be improved?
- Should I consider factoring?
- Where are they wasting money?

Staff meeting

Depending on the business, the staff can be a significant part of what you are buying. The problem being that staff, however valuable they may be to the enterprise, are free to resign at any time. They cannot be made to stay by law or contract, but they can be motivated to stay. The question therefore that you really want to ask is: 'If I was to be the new boss of this business would you stay, leave, or wait to see what the new change brings?' If your coming in brings new investment with it then they are likely to benefit significantly from the transition. For staff expansion brings opportunities for career progression.

As you don't own the business yet and it is a going concern, you have to be very diplomatic in meeting staff. Often vendors will quite reasonably not let you meet the staff to protect confidentiality until terms and legal matters have progressed significantly.

You have to be able to make a judgement; are they the sort of people you feel you could lead? What are their hopes, frustrations and ambitions? Sometimes you will have to judge this from an overall impression of how they respond, their body language, work atmosphere, how they react to each other.

If there are really key staff, it is possible to bring them into a deal by agreeing with the vendor that he/she will pay a loyalty bonus after the staff stay with you for say six months after completion. Other ways might be improving packages or offering a share incentive scheme.

On a technical note, if you are buying just the business assets and goodwill, not the shares of a company, then in the UK the transfer of undertakings of employment legislation (TUPE) will apply. This means that all staff contracts are assigned to you as they stand automatically on purchase. Please refer to your legal advisors for more detail. In particular there may be an obligation to consult with the staff about the transaction, which clearly has implications for both buyer and seller. There is a particular obligation to consult if you intend to change terms on purchase.

Due diligence checklist

The due diligence process is a fact-find mission or survey designed to ensure that the representations being made by the sellers are true, and that the business is sustainable without hidden liabilities. Buyers should be wary however. The past is not a guide to the future and as many questions should be asked in the due diligence process about 'what next' as they are about the past. Indeed, the most positive way to undertake the due diligence process is not just to check the business, but also to use it as a very real part of the future of the business, forming a base for business planning. This double whammy approach also gains the most value out of it. Instead of a survey to cross the T's that ends up in a drawer, the process can identify weaknesses and threats, all of which present opportunity and challenge.

The idea of due diligence is, as the name implies, to diligently check all aspects of the business. In particular, if shares are being bought the new shareholders will inherit all previous liability whether known or otherwise. Indeed, this is why most buyers would prefer to just buy the assets from the company rather than shares, however usually this makes the tax position untenable for the seller. Liabilities for previous activities such as environmental issues or revenue claims are typical, and although these can be warranted and indemnified (financially guaranteed by the seller) in the legal contract it is still much better to be aware of what you are getting into. The due diligence process also helps as issues identified can form the basis of extra covenants to include in the legal contracts to manage the risks associated with a deal.

The due diligence formally starts when you have reached an agreement on principle on the purchase and you will now be inspecting all of the records. Eventually you will find out all its secrets, but you want that to be before you buy. Make sure you are not put under pressure during this period. Do all the checking you need to do before progressing. Your due diligence checking should cover every aspect of the business. The vendor should allow you and your advisors access to do so. Anything they don't want to give you access to, be wary over, although respect that there is certain key information they may need to keep to the last point to protect the goodwill until contracts are nearly agreed.

It is entirely possible for a buyer to do much of the initial due diligence work themselves, however it is a very in depth job and the benefit of employing a skilled professional to produce a report is they should have significant experience of what to look for. All corporate lawyers and most accountants can help in some way and they should be insured for the job. Most corporations will have someone internally who can help them manage the process. Don't assume the professional will find out everything 100%, its your money you are spending after all. Double-check and double-check again and use your common sense. Also make sure if using a professional you manage your costs.

If the due diligence process shows the business in a bad light either drop the price or, failing that, walk away. We recommend breaking the process into 5 areas. The following is a basic initial list and not intended to be exhaustive. The cultural one is an unusual fifth, however, as in a recent survey over 70% of Chief Executives felt that their acquisitions underperformed and they identified cultural reasons as the biggest contributor. Their two organizations just did not on reflection understand each other.

Legal	**Financial**	**Commercial**	**Property**	**Cultural**
Employee contracts, personnel files	Files on pensions, profit shares or bonus payments	Registered brand names, patents or copyrights	Health and safety	Management style
Any commitment/ promises to any supplier or customer or staff	Any seasonality in sales or customers over 10% of business	Complaints	Environment assessment	Age and length of service
Any potential claims – environmental, employees	Asset valuations and resale values – fixed asset register	Pricing policy and terms and conditions to customers	Copies of leases	Past track record
Memorandum and Articles of Incorporation	Stock ordering and levels	Marketing files, including brochures and web page	Schedule of any dilapidations	Staff ambitions and aims
Minutes of Board of Directors, Committee and Shareholder meetings	Tax and VAT policies	Brand and press profile	Property surveys	Staff policies, holidays, cars expenses culture

Legal	Financial	Commercial	Property	Cultural
Details of current shareholders and other interests in the company	Insurance		Site plans	
Overviews of any pending legal cases	Bank guarantees and charges			
All contracts, customer staff	Aged debtor creditor list			
	3 years accounts			
	Accounts projections/ cashflow forecasts			
	Management accounts			

In summary the aims of the due diligence process can be to:

- Ascertain the true value of the business and that the right price is to be paid.
- Identify hidden or potential liabilities to be managed in the legal contract.
- Find hidden profit and opportunities.
- Ensure there are no cultural clashes with your plans or organization.
- Make sure that all facts are being disclosed and the vendor and their advisor are telling it how it is.

Potential purchase timetable

	Responsibility	Item	Month					
			1	2	3	4	5	6
1	Board/Me	Identify your strategy	•					
2	Board	Choose professional advisors (see note below)	•					
3		Research	•					
4	Appointed head of project	Contact Brokers	•					
5		Potentially employ acquisition advisor to help with research, valuation and negotiation	•					
6		Look at direct approaches	•					
7		Shortlist prospects	•					
8		Agree confidentially	•					
9		Provide within reason initial information on your financial position/reason for interest	•					
10		Obtain key financial, business information	•					
11		Analyze business information	•					
12		Visit vendor		•				
13		Assess vendor		•				
14		Checklist against your buying criteria		•				
15		Does it match now, or can it with potential		•				
16		Identify objectively its value to you		•				
17		Research funding options if serious to assess your ability to finance		•				
18		Negotiate hard but non adversarial		•				
19		Listen to vendor			•			
20		Wait if they don't accept	As required					
21		Agree heads of terms (exchange of letters outlining key points of your agreement subject to contract, to create clarity and avoid moving goal posts)				•		
22		Apply for funding				•		
23		Instruct lawyers				•		
24		Seek regulatory approval if required				•		
25		Set target for completion				•		
26		Carry out due diligence and instruct advisors to help				•	•	
27		Negotiate with legal advisors definitive sale contract					•	
28		Manage lawyers/advisors to completion						•

Note: Good professional advisors will help you free with initial research if you go and see them, and undertake to use them as you progress matters. Most offer 30 minutes free advice if you approach them in the right way. Be careful not to employ them unless you have specific need.

chapter six Business planning – Mapping the way

SIX Business planning – Mapping the way

"You can't just ask customers what they want and then try to give that to them. By the time you get it built, they'll want something new."

Steve Jobs

"Anybody can cut prices, but it takes brains to produce a better article."

H. Ross Perot

"To climb steep hills requires slow pace at first."

William Shakespeare

Chapter focus

This chapter will outline the importance of a written plan when starting or buying a business. Management guides for business planning are plentiful. Here we concentrate on the overall project from start-up or purchase to the planned eventual sale for capital wealth.

- **Introduction**
- **Why you must write a plan**
- **What should be in your plan?**
- **Raising finance**
- **Types of finance**
- **Planning tips**
- **From start to finish**
- **Business plan template – start to finish**

Introduction

For buying, starting up and selling a business for capital gain there are three phases to the project, bounded by:

- Where are you now?
- The starting point, and where do you want to be?
- The end point.

This requires analysis and planning. In this chapter therefore we take an overview of the business planning process and outline its importance when starting or developing a business. There are many definitive texts on the subject in particular for start-ups. We aim to give an insight only with a particular focus on the individual entrepreneur and the planned eventual sale for capital wealth.

Why you must write a plan

There is an old saying, 'You get what you focus on'. The key to success then is to make sure that you focus on exactly what you want. Can you explain your business objectives to someone that you were passing, in opposite directions, on an elevator? When you have it that precise, you have the necessary pinpoint focus. Business planning is a powerful and vital tool aimed at getting this focus, yet it is often under-utilized, probably because there are some persuasive excuses. These include:

- We only need a plan to secure funding.
- Time spent planning gets in the way of time spent doing. We achieve more if we do.
- Markets and business change rapidly so plans are out of date before we even start.
- Plans are rarely stuck to.

As these excuses are so persuasive why do we still recommend plans, particularly in increasingly changing markets? It only works if you think of a plan as a constant reference map. Imagine you are choosing to circumnavigate the world. You will have specific staging points, however as you get near to these destinations the weather, political issues, even sometimes quicker methods of transport might be found.

So as you progress you adapt your journey, even change your staging points. You need your original plan in mind so that even if you are completely off track, you know where you are relative to where you want to be. Better still, you have the overall map and the grand vision of completing the circumnavigation.

The mistake most people make with plans is seeing them as inflexible. This is probably due to the time they invest in them. The thought process is, "I am investing all this time in developing the plan so I must stick to it." They do a plan, fail to stick to it and therefore never do another one. If we think of planning differently however, we should not expect plans to be rigid. After all, when did any military strategy go according to plan once the enemy had been engaged? New strategies and tactics are developed to react to the enemy's move and it is embracing this concept that ensures the military victory. We see business plans as organic and adapting journeys. The plan is the map with clearly marked starting and end points.

Plans help by:

- Establishing the destination. If you know exactly where you want to go you have more chance of getting there.
- Defining the steps involved to get to the destination. If you break a big destination into obvious easy steps it becomes easier to hit each individual goal, where as the grand plan can be too big and intimidating.
- Providing a working document of your vision. This can be used to persuade financiers, and staff to back you and help you lead them.
- Creating focus and clarity. Both increase productivity and drive at goals.
- Create an active and objective look at the business (or start-up idea). This forces real analysis and ensures potential problems are identified and addressed.
- Provide an 'acid test' with a range of questions. This ensures all risks, logistics and opportunities are explored, and contingency plans established.
- Creating a clear reference point. This helps you make decisions, and analyze as you reflect on progress.
- Establishing focus. This removes distraction.

What should be in your plan?

If we were reviewing a plan to consider supporting it, here is a list of what we would want answers to. Make sure that you have covered all these points. Show your plan to other business people and seek their opinion.

Business and market		✓
1	Does the business concept make sense?	
2	Is there at least one unique and valuable competitive advantage?	
3	Is anything new being offered?	
4	Has competition been taken seriously enough?	
5	Who are the competitors?	
6	Is it possible to dominate or lead the sector?	
7	Is their potential to create a new market and thus lead it?	
8	Are there barriers of entry working for or against the plan?	
9	What are market conditions in this or similar sectors?	
10	Have all risks and opportunities been fully considered?	
11	Is a recession likely?	
12	What are the main pcssible threats and are they prepared for?	
Development		✓
13	Are the management skills in place to achieve the plan?	
14	What do you need to invest in the business as soon as you arrive?	
15	Are there clear added values from the introduction of the new owner/manager?	
16	Detail plans of changes that could be made to improve the business over time (never rush them – get a feel for the business first)	
17	Are there resources that are currently unexploited?	

Money		✓
18	Do the accounts stack up? Are they realistic whilst still appealing?	
19	Is there finance in place or a realistic method to raise finance?	
20	How will any finance you are requesting support the plan?	
21	What is the cost of the start-up or business being purchased?	
22	Is the potential return on the investment worth the risk?	
23	Have taxation considerations been fully considered?	
24	Are financial projections and aims realistic?	
25	Is significant growth dependent on significant capital injection?	
Lending criteria		✓
26	Are projections realistic and achievable? What are the risks of things going wrong and what happens if they do?	
27	Is the proposal able to service and repay the debt?	
28	Does the proposal generate adequate cash flow to service both the interest and capital elements of the requested debt? (Although profits are important, cash flow projections are also vital.)	
29	Do financial ratios such as gearing, interest cover and asset cover look appropriate?	
30	What security is available for the proposed lending in order to limit their exposure should the development plans go badly wrong? Is the value and quality of the security sufficient? (Banks may seek to improve their security position by requesting personal guarantees.)	

Management		✓
31	Is the new owner/manager personally committed and tied in?	
32	Is the new owner tough, practical, skilled and experienced enough to make it happen?	
31	Has the new entrepreneur done their homework on the market?	
31	Is there any expertise needed which is not present?	
32	Is this an industry where the business value is in the staff employed?	
31	How can the staff be locked in? Will they be loyal?	
32	Who else is backing this plan?	
Exit route		✓
33	Is the exit strategy realistic?	
34	Will it be at a favourable time?	
35	Who are the potential buyers?	
36	Would it be better to build the business more before selling?	
37	Is the exit strategy flexible enough to pick a high in the market?	
38	How does this affect the capital value?	

As part of the process carry out a SWOT plan. Below is a basic example.

Strengths	Weaknesses	Opportunities	Threats
My management skills	Time taken up looking at potential businesses	Market conditions allow buying at a discount with a market upturn on the horizon	Competing bids for a target business
My negotiating skill	Investment is not asset-backed	Clients brought in	Recession affecting whole of industry
My industry knowledge	Dependence on ongoing bank support	My innovative marketing ideas to apply to the industry	High dependence on key staff
My industry contacts for an eventual sale of the business	I have minimal cash funds to see through any unexpected lean period	For a start up, spotted a clear gap in the market	For a start up, risk in gaining initial customer as per budgeted timescale
Funds available	For a start up, formula not proven		

Raising finance

When buying or starting up a business funding is a crucial issue. Producing a plan will help ensure that the funding requirement is justifiable, affordable and that the business proposal is achievable. There are many reasons for requiring business funding. Typically these might include:

- Acquisitions
- Capital expenditure
- Working capital
- Restructuring
- New product and/or market development

The type of finance appropriate will depend on the level of funding required. The amount of funds required will dictate the costs of the process. When considering funding requirements, also build a contingency in case forecasts are not achieved. Very serious consideration should be given to how justifiable the commercial requirement for funding is. Such consideration can also help you understand the most appropriate type of finance suitable to you and should include:

- How risky is the business proposal?
- What will the proposal achieve for the business?
- What level of borrowing is appropriate for the business?
- Is a dilution in ownership necessary and acceptable?
- What are the long-term plans of management?
- What operational and financial constraints are acceptable?
- What are the exit routes available?

The argument goes that if it is a good business opportunity then there will always be someone who is prepared to finance it, to share in the gains. This is usually true, but it can take a while to locate and secure suitable funds. There are many ways to finance and we outline the main ones here.

Raising finance from any source leverages your potential opportunity. It develops you from someone with say £40,000 to invest to someone with £200,000 to invest, thus giving you access to opportunities that would not otherwise be open to you, and a potential much higher capital gain level.

Ask who has, or could have an interest in me being successful. If you are going to employ more people the government will have various schemes to help you, not just in terms of direct finance but also in offering services free of charge or at much reduced rates. If you want to export for example, there are schemes that will pay your flights abroad and set up contacts on a trade mission for you. Contact your local Chamber of Commerce, Small Firms Service or bank manager.

One aspect you need to think about carefully is pledging assets as security and giving personal guarantees. Just because a financier might ask for them or even have them in their pre-printed agreements, do not automatically accept them. Bank managers and factorers do offer their services without personal guarantees or securities. Negotiate hard. If you give a personal guarantee and sell the business the commitment could still be in place. If you take on the lease of say an office, when you sell on, if the new owner defaults the liability will probably revert back to you. So before you sign anything be sure of all the commitments that it ties you to! Your job when running a business is to manage both the fixed costs and the contingent liabilities.

Lending terms will depend on the type, risk and security of the proposal, so rate conditions and periods vary significantly. Typically for short and medium-term finance interest rates are generally between 1% and 4% over base.

Financial planning is a specialist job. As there are advisers that help with business planning, many can also assist with raising the funds for your venture. Good advisers can really help here, even down to getting the right bank. Be careful however to research whom you use in depth. Hasty and ill-informed decisions will result in failure. Make sure you are clear with your finance-planning adviser of your objectives and manage costs. Get it in writing and, where possible, the majority of fees contingent on success.

Types of finance and terms

There are many different types of finance including:

Short-term debt: Usually suitable for working capital requirements and short-term fluctuations often financed by overdrafts and as such are repayable on demand.

Long-term finance: Typically provided by banks. Medium (3-5 years) and long-term (over 5 years) loans are usually required to finance longer term requirements such as capital expenditure or elements of an acquisition. Normally, subject to a loan agreement, where security is taken over assets.

Specialist asset financiers: Usually arranged by specialist firms often affiliated with banks. Lending can be short-term such as invoice discounting or factoring. Alternatively, for significant business developments operational leasing or hire purchase finance can be used for medium or long-term funds. The key concern for such lenders is the quality of the assets that they are lending against and if they provide adequate security.

Venture and development capital

- Venture capitalists normally require an annual compound return of between 25% and 60%, depending on their perceived risk of the investment. This equates, for a return requirement of 35%, to £1,000 today 'costing' £4,500 over a five-year period.
- Preference shares enable a lower equity shareholding despite the size of their relative investment. They are often required to be redeemed once allowed by the company's profits and cash flows.
- Venture capitalists can be relatively flexible regarding dividend payments reflecting projected profitability and cash requirement.

Equity finance: Typically where a business contact, friends or family agree to support the venture in return for equity in the business. There are many high net worth individuals' known as business angels who will invest in smaller companies, particularly ones that qualify for tax relief.

Finance method	Advantages	Disadvantages
Vendor financing	Vested interest in backing you Commits him to belief in business to finance payments. Probably best terms.	Difficult to offer security to vendor Can, under current legislation, trigger complications in company using its own money to buy itself (financial assistance) Vendors not ready lenders.
Own cash	Good for putting down a deposit to seal the deal No interest payments or other partners to consider Total control	Ties up your liquid resources Reduces cash security in times of crisis Requires family's approval Loss of interest
Secured bank loan	Attractive interest rates Tax deductible, as all business interest	Interest payments put burden on the business Bank manager will want regular reports and will have a say in the management Security on for example your house puts it at risk
Unsecured bank loan	No security, however lenders will still pursue payment of any default.	Need good credit record and convincing argument to secure Higher interest rates Personal guarantees usually required

Finance method	Advantages	Disadvantages
Factoring (raising funds by advancing money on debtors)	Releases money tied up in sales and as a 'secured' finance is more readily available Offers credit control facilities	Be wary of small print on deals, particularly personal guarantees Reduces margin on sales often significantly. Customers see that you have raised funds on your invoice to them You lose control of debt collection
Invoice discounting	As above	As above without disadvantage of customers seeing you have raised funds against their future payment
Business angel	Investment for shares means no interest burden May come with valuable expertise and contacts	Reduced equity ownership Partner will want a say in the running of the business Often much time in finding partner(s)
Friends and family	Similar to business angel	Personal commitment hard to walk away from if anything should go wrong
Venture capitalist	Suitable more for Management Buy In, or for larger deals They will want to see clear business plan with substantial growth prospects and clear exit routes Will offer equity and loan finance mix	Equity partners will want a seat on the board Be wary of small print of any deal Can take a lot of time and effort to raise
Leasing	Suitable for vehicles, or equipment	Long-term commitment with penalties for early surrender
Grants	Free money Might be available from government or EEC sources	Time and energy in researching current opportunities with no certainty of success
Special loan Schemes (such as UK Government's Small Firms Loan Guarantee Scheme)	Special favourable terms and application criterion apply	None, unless perhaps difficult to secure if you already have access to money

Planning tips

Business planning is a big subject and there is a lot involved. Being prepared and understanding the process can save a lot of time, so a bit of research before you start is extremely helpful. On the Internet there are many resources on writing business plans, including free templates. Start looking on the sites of business angels, banks and venture capitalists. In the UK www.3i.com is the largest venture capital firm and a good starting point. There are also specialists who can help you including Avondale Group (Kevin's firm) but remember a good advisor will help you create your plan and make sure it is effective. They are not responsible for whether it is viable. That is one of your sole roles and should NEVER be delegated even if someone else helps with producing the plan.

There are two aspects to making capital wealth from buying/starting and selling a business. One is to start from scratch or buy at a low price and sell at a premium. The other is to add value to the business by what you bring. The best way of course is to do both. To do this effectively you need to develop your skills at assessing a business's potential, calculating a worthwhile purchase price, when the potential is clear, and then negotiating a price below this. If you can buy it for a figure below this you clearly have a bargain. Bring both these elements into the planning process and:

- at every step have in mind the effects of each stage on capital value;
- detail your end point, the exit route.

Other tips include:

Avoid perfection: A business plan can have so many aspects and be changing so much the process can very easily become all time consuming. Don't get obsessive and perfectionist.

Share your plan: A plan can help you and your people focus on achieving your goals. It must not get in the way of them. Staff that are busy on the phone talking to customers will not see you writing a plan all day as demonstrating leadership. Do it after working hours at the weekend, when there are no interruptions, or create quiet time. If you are in an established team tell people what you are undertaking and ask for their help and opinions.

Use your plan: A good business plan is not a lot of use if it just rests in a filing cabinet. It is a working document to be referred to and worked on regularly. For example, the cash flow forecast should be referred to on a weekly basis, warning of any potential problem. Share and circulate your plan for opinions.

Ask every day "How can I make this business better?" Writing a good plan is initially about gathering information. If you ask questions, of yourself, your team and your customers, you will get answers. The trick therefore is to ask the right questions.

From start to finish

Until now we have tried to address a broad audience, although always with the entrepreneur or owner in mind. There are specifics to consider depending on whether you are starting from scratch or buying a business, also depending on which step you are at. In particular, care and thought should be given to planning the exit well ahead as your chosen time comes to the horizon.

The start up: If you are starting a business from scratch, then a written plan is even more important. A new business will probably have products, services, branding and market demand all based on what you think and hope it will be. There are no historic files to give you customer feedback. There is no proof that your way of doing business will work. The business idea has not yet proved it can make a sale. The business model has not proved it can one day operate at a profit. Risk is therefore far greater, and the way to minimize this is to write down a plan addressing every area of the projected business and why you think it will work. Be careful of wishful thinking, or of finding only evidence that backs up your point of view. Make it a point to play devil's advocate on your own plan. Then get close friends with business experience to try and find holes in it. Challenge them to find at least three faults.

As any project manager knows, the first stages of any project are the most crucial. This investment can save you a fortune in time and money avoiding problems before you start. It should also give you a reasonably accurate figure for the start-up capital you will need and how much finance the business will require until cash receipts overtake cash outlays.

For the start-up, once you are in business cash flow is vital; profit and loss is in the future. You are in a race to stop the cash haemorrhaging. This is the area where most business start-ups greatly underestimate the time it will take to establish new sales. Then how long it will take sales to turn into cash. It is also why we prefer the purchase route.

However, most of the richest entrepreneurs in the world started from scratch, so don't let us put you off if you have a great unique innovative idea, with commercial potential.

The purchase: Before making an offer, think about all the things that could go wrong and address them to your satisfaction, and put them in your plan. You should also have in mind your exit strategy. This can range from immediately putting it back on the market to building up over 3-5 years. Whatever your objectives it is best to focus on them early on, and work back, step by step, to what you have to do.

If you are an individual entrepreneur identify your own personal timescales for your life plan, including where you want to go next and what you want to do with the capital gain. You need a compelling reason to help maintain your momentum, motivation and drive throughout the project.

Pre-acquisition: On acquiring a business most buyers will want to develop the business, particularly if they are seeking a long-term capital gain. This agenda should be borne in mind pre-acquisition planning and at the due diligence (checking the target company is as good as it appears) stage. Buyers should be cautious not to over-estimate the changes they can make in the short-term. Sometimes too much change too quickly can damage existing revenue streams and at worst alienate the staff force that could be crucial to on-going success. Culture differences and failure to plan change management are cited as the biggest reason for unsuccessful acquisitions.

Many due diligence investigations are shelved post-acquisition but clever buyers will use this checking process as a route map to create effective business plans. Think of it as a house survey detailing the weak spots in the property that need tidying up for a nice house, but also to increase its saleability.

Some pre-acquisition business planning questions might include, how can I...

- Increase profits?
- Improve margins?
- Increase sales and order size?
- Control costs?
- Create better systems?
- Ensure improved productivity?

Questions for the team might include:

- Are they motivated?
- Are they motivated consistently?
- Do they work well as a team?
- Do they need training in sales skills?
- Could they use a better approach?
- What ideas do they have?
- Are they targeting the right market?
- Do their incentives need reviewing?
- Questions for the marketing approach might include:
- What do customers like about us?
- What could we get them to buy more of?
- What would have to happen for them to order more?
- Are there extra services we could sell them?
- Should we be looking at special offers of some kind?
- Do we need to look at sales promotion?
- Should we increase advertising?
- Should we change our advertising media?
- Should we conduct some market research?
- Should we have a website?
- Should we look at overseas opportunities?
- What trends in our industry look like they will grow soon?

We don't believe there is a small business out there that could seriously ask all of the above questions and not find more opportunities for sales. Ask them, make changes and then ask them again.

The exit plan: Identify three years ahead when you intend to sell and start working early with your professional advisors towards this goal. A successful exit is all about planning and your advisors are your coaches to ensure you win.

Business plan template

The following simplistic outline covers an initial note from buying, value adding through to selling. It is intended largely to help clarify your ideas and why you think there is money to be made. Obviously, until a specific business is purchased there are no report and accounts to analyze and project into the future. Once in a business a more detailed plan should be undertaken, with three to five years of projected Cash Flow Forecasts, P/L Accounts and Balance Sheet. We have included several books and web pages, including our own that offer further useful tools.

John Smith Business Plan

To buy out a *(Type of Business Here)*

Add value and double profits and then sell in *(number of)* years on for double the purchase price.

Phase 1: Search and Purchase of Suitable Enterprise (or start-up)

Phase 2: Add Value, Expand

Phase 3: Sell, Realize Capital Gain

Contents

- Executive summary
- Financial
- Opportunity sought
- Value added
- Market assessment
- Exit route
- Timescale of action plan

Executive summary:

Overall synopsis of plan to exploit opportunities.

Financial

Own cash available	**A**
+Friends and family	**B**
+Possible bank finance	**C**
+Other, including business angel	**D**
+Debtor factoring/equipment HP	**E**
Total own resources	**£F**
Vendor financing (if buying?)	**£G**
Total funds available	**£H**
Apportioned:	
Purchase finance	**£I**
Initial development fund	**£J**

Opportunity sought

Criterion:

Industry sector(s):	xxxxxxxx
Location(s)	xxxxxxxx
Price range	xxxxxxxx
Maximum multiple paid	x
Vendor financing	x%
Other	

Value Added

Me, specifically A

Clients brought in B

Marketing innovations C

Other innovations D

Synergies E

Economies of scale F

Key staff brought in G

Market assessment

A review and appraisal of the market and its competitors and its strengths, weaknesses, opportunities and threats.

Strengths:

Weaknesses:

Opportunities:

Threats:

Exit route

To put on market as soon as profit levels are doubled, with a three year target. At this time I predict the market will be more buoyant than now and we can achieve a better multiple than what we paid and achieve full value. We will put it with a broker and also I will approach personal contacts in the industry that could be interested in expanding their businesses.

Take tax and financial advice early on through a professional intermediary. Manage process to completion via intermediary.

Timescale of action plan

Year 1, Qtr 1: First quarter from now

Search and review businesses through brokers, and negotiate a deal that meets all criterion.

Year 1, Qtr 1: First quarter as new owner

Establish my leadership and motivate staff to new vision

Get to know/meet each staff member

Meet main customers

Bring in initial first clients

Complete full business plan from actual historic accounts

Use costs as budgets and sales as targets to staff

Make contingency plans for everything that could go wrong (Main customer pulls out, competitor opens up locally, key staff resign, bank calls in overdraft)

Design all staff bonuses to beating budget

Formalize marketing plan

Review all overheads

Review IT/computer systems

Year 1 Qtr 2,3,4

Develop online marketing

Work all hours to develop sales

Consider how to lock in key staff, including share options

Track and analyze 6 key competitors' activities

Increase operating efficiency in all processes

Write operating manual for all processes

Make marketing investment

Growth plan actioned

Year 2

Continue to raise sales

Establish niche and branding

Continue to improve operating efficiencies

Year 3, 4,

Appoint experienced sale intermediary

Reduce long-term investment costs

Taper off recruitment to replace only

Increase training spend

Develop current customers rather than seek new business

Year 5

Bring any litigation, conflicts or disputes to a close, even if it means compromise

Ensure no debts left outstanding over 30 days

Ensure no unpaid creditors over 60 days

Cut expenditure on non-core activities

Make initial approaches to potential buyers

Year 6

"Plans are only good intentions unless they immediately degenerate into hard work."

Peter Drucker

chapter seven Adding value – Acorns into oaks

SEVEN Adding value – Acorns into oaks

"Never spend your money before you have it."

Thomas Jefferson

"I try to keep in touch with the details... I also look at the product daily. That doesn't mean you interfere, but it's important occasionally to show the ability to be involved. It shows you understand what's happening."

Rupert Murdoch

Chapter focus

The key areas that offer opportunities for adding the most value to a business, with practical ideas on how to groom a business for maximum sale value, minimizing risk and cost in the process.

- **Introduction**
- **Working in and on the business**
- **Adding value by the hour**
- **Stand out**
- **Create barriers to entry**
- **Pre-sale grooming**
- **Tips and techniques for adding value**
- **Summary**

Introduction

Most business owner's focus purely on profit, and as a bi-product therefore create capital or shareholder value. We contend that it is possible to work on both and increase both at the same time. Many of the aspects are similar and the trick is to think about both as you go along. In this chapter we look at what (aside from making more money) adds value to a business. In the mergers and acquisition world this is known as sale grooming or creating shareholder value. The good news about many grooming aspects is that they are, in our opinion, good business practice anyway, and you don't always have to apply them as a prelude to sale. They can be used to give you the choice to sell, which when you face the decision you may choose not to.

Many will look at our wish list of grooming or adding value ideas below, and say it's too much. On the surface we can see why, however it is important to remember that little changes really will make a big difference. We believe in 'Kaizen', a Japanese management principle that advocates in a sustainable business the best way to improve it is continuous, and that small changes in every area add up to a big difference. Imagine a 10% improvement in your training, delegation, customer loyalty, systems, marketing, buying arrangements, office presentation, accounts management etc, all might add up to 100% increase in business.

One of the grooming areas to concentrate on is branding. We consider this so important we have devoted the next chapter just to this area.

Working on and in the business

Where possible for the majority of owner/managers the best way to grow a business for profit and capital value is to work on the business, not in it. This does two things; it removes the owner from doing a job that is skilled and irreplaceable on sale, it also ensures the focus and time is being spent on achieving growth.

Working **on** the business means to be outside looking at strategic issues and improvements. Working **in** is getting involved in the day to day operations and doing the 'skilled job'. For example, if you are an Estate Agent that has opened your own office, if you are selling houses all day you are working in the business using your professional skills. Your sales and negotiation skills are your goodwill. If on the other hand you are reviewing costs, grooming it for a sale, recruiting, developing its potential then you are working on the business. Whilst this is a skilled job, it is replaceable, after all many of the buyers may have departments just to work on the business.

Many owners struggle to work on the business; they keep getting dragged into the job. This is in part because of the character of the owner/manager which can be control-orientated. The short-sighted see doing the job as control and therefore they 'do it themselves', after all no one else can do it as well! The successful owner/manager will break this mode, eventually realizing that control is an illusion and that what can be achieved is best obtained through systems, procedures, training, effective delegation, strong recruitment and clarity of goals.

The more an owner works on a business, the better its infrastructure systems, brand and concept. This means even if its profits are still similar to before, it is worth more, as there is far more of a base to expand from; the business is a more reliable, stable and sustainable platform. It is also probably much easier to take over. The acquirer's ideal purchase is a business that has a track record of growth, further potential and a strong platform to leverage this potential including quality people. If you score in all these areas you will achieve a higher multiple on your profits than a comparable profit business with no scope and in need of modernization. Interestingly, seven out of ten venture capitalists now rate the quality of management as equally or more important than the product in assessing a business's likely success potential.

Whilst we are advocating work on the business approach to maximize its value, we should urge caution that occasionally it is beneficial to go back to the shop floor and work in the business. This is to find out what staff, customers and suppliers really think of your business.

Adding value by the hour

Quite often businesses that first come available for sale are hampered for further growth because the originator does not want to let go of control and decision-making power. If tasks that you are doing do not require your expertise then they should be considered for delegation. You have got to cost yourself on an hourly basis.

Whatever your business, if you are looking to build it and sell it for a capital gain within five years then you have to add value hourly. Do not kid yourself that you are being thrifty by doing a variety of tasks yourself to save the money. Most small businesses are under capitalized (many owners fail to recognize this too), which means that you have to maximize the productivity of every resource. The main asset of your business is you. If you had a million pound machine you would want it working at top productivity, would you not? Every time you do something that does not add value at £50 per hour plus you have lost the opportunity of adding value at £100 per hour. Ask yourself what else you could be doing which is more important/valuable.

One way to assess your approach and cost yourself effectively is by doing a time cost log. Take a piece of paper and on the left hand side write a list of all the activities you and each staff member does. When you have completed this, on the right hand side write what you think the hourly added value is to the business of you doing this work. When you have completed this, re-write the list in order of lowest value to highest value. You now have a piece of paper clearly showing you what you need to seriously consider delegating in priority order. You can also extend this exercise to all your staff. Here is an example from someone who manages a travel agency:

Deleting junk e-mails	£3 per hour
Opening the post	£3
Buying the stationary	£5
General office management	£6
Surfing the Internet	£6
Answering letters	£8
Attending trade fairs	£9
Accounting	£15
Meeting key suppliers	£30
Answering incoming calls	£40
Organizing computer systems	£45
Staff training	£50
Recruitment	£55
Marketing	£60
Developing operational efficiency	£65

Grooming	£65
Managing cash flow	£75
Information technology (IT) development	£100
Meeting customers	£100
Sales	£100
Reviewing/reducing costs	£100
Leadership and motivating staff	£200
Strategic business planning and implementation	£225

Of course this list is subjective and will vary given the nature of each individual business, and the business cycle which it is undertaking. When you look closer at each item you may find it breaks down further, into parts that add different values to the enterprise. It is also important to consider your own expertise. If you are no good at IT, but have a heavy IT-dependent business, you might rate it higher on the hourly scale but still choose to delegate it. In this case the importance will be on whom to delegate it and making sure it is effective delegation.

Stand out

The market leader or the threat to it is the most valuable business in its sector. Differentiating yourself from your competitors by establishing a core area of strength within your market sector or, in marketing speak, creating unique selling points will increase the desirability of your business to buyers. This in turn will increase the price that buyers will be prepared to pay. A well-marketed business will generate a 'we need/we want' motivation in buyers.

Intensify your marketing strategy to raise the company's profile. Create a culture and/or a brand that provides you with customer and staff loyalty. Thorn EMI paid a staggering £593 million for Virgin Music Group in 1992, a sum of several times any traditional valuation.

Remember that little changes to a company can make big differences to its market value. So buy, start up or develop a company that is geared up for where its future market will be, one that offers potential to stand out. Standing out and developing a brand is such an important aspect of adding value to a business we have devoted the whole of the next chapter to go into this in more depth.

Create barriers to entry

A barrier to entry, as the term suggests is something that prevents a potential competitor from entering your market. Clearly, such a barrier is very nice to have and will increase your value, and not so nice to come up against. Giving thought to this area and how to create barriers to entry can help you add value to your business. Your competitors may even be forced to buy you to get rid of the barrier to enable their expansion.

We can divide barriers into several categories:

1. Established market share

Having an established market share implies that you have a degree of brand awareness and customer loyalty. The barrier can be broken down when competitors find better solutions to your customers' needs.

2. Intellectual property

Copyright, patents, trademarks. If your product has a patent on it then no one can legally reach that market with the same product. Inventions or innovations can cover any aspect of the business, a product, a process or a service style.

3. Customer service

It is not just how good your service is, but the way that you do it. Dominos for example are effectively in the same business as Perfect Pizza or Pizza House; however there moped delivery service makes them stand out. If a business has a loyal customer for whatever reason, this constitutes a barrier for a competitor to enter the market.

4. Strategic partnerships (and contracts)

If a company has an exclusive relationship with a customer or supplier for example, this can be a barrier to entry if it gives clear advantages. Microsoft's relationship with major PC manufacturers and retailers is an example of this. In several industries it is common to find Preferred Supplier Lists in operation, which is obviously a barrier.

In the business there are always some things you must have, and some you need not. Challenging these can lead to new ideas. For example, a barrier to entry might be two retail bookstores fighting for the top spot in a town and not allowing room for a third. Amazon challenging the need for retail units cut straight through this.

Pre-sale grooming

In the above we talk about general ways to add value to your business, however there are a few practical specific actions that can be carried out in advance once a business sale strategy has been chosen, preferably some time before the anticipated sale date. These actions do not solely relate to profitability but include reducing uncertainty, complications and risk to the acquirer. These actions are best reviewed and undertaken with the advice and help of a professional sale intermediary, preferably two to three years before sale. The following are the more common areas for attention.

Commercial

Tidy up

Present the business in the best possible light. This may mean tidy offices, or designing a smart corporate brochure or web site. Produce both to serve customers. Clear filing systems and smart staff will also help. Information technology is also a good area to look at. Are your systems reliable, up to date and fully licensed?

Management

We have already discussed that your role needs to be replaceable. The stronger and more informed your team around you, the easier it is for a buyer to take over. Delegate where possible and create clear areas of accountability and responsibility to quality people around you. The more established and sustainable the team the happier the buyer will be.

Reduce dependency on key customers or suppliers

Dependency can, on occasion, significantly reduce marketability of the business, especially where there is a close relationship with the owner. If you have such a dependency slowly introduce other staff to the client and focus on bringing in new business as well. Imagine, what is the worst letter you could get on your desk the next day? It could be from key staff or a key customer severing your arrangements. Ask what you can do to mitigate this risk.

Environmental health and safety issues

Ensure the company possesses all appropriate licenses and complies with all required procedures. Ensure environmental concerns associated with the business premises, production process or products are understood and minimized. An environmental audit may be appropriate to establish areas of concern. A similar review should be undertaken for the health and safety aspects of the company.

Create a culture

Businesses like people have characteristics. There are some that are stuck in their ways, inflexible and lack imagination. They are out of touch and ignorant. If your business has any of these aspects, break them. Create a culture of knowledge, teamwork and change. Buyers will not take on your business unless they feel that they can work with your business and its people. We mention earlier that the biggest reason cited for failed acquisitions is a failure to integrate/understand the culture. If your staff are not used to change, how will they handle a sale? Buyers will sense this and avoid the business.

Legal

Formalize and review contracts

Review trading, employment and agency agreements to ensure they are transferable to a new owner. Consider if there are any renewals that will have an impact on sale and time the sale accordingly or renegotiate these arrangements prior to sale. Are there any personal guarantees, or charges on personal assets given by you to finance the business or provide comfort to landlords? Buyers will have to replace these, so if you can negotiate out of them now you will increase the value to them and make a sale easier. Ensure the company possesses all appropriate licenses and complies with all required procedures. Have you got all your software licences?

Employees

Final salary pension schemes can be extremely unwieldy at a sale so these need looking at early on and establishing the true position. Other than that do you comply with the working time-directive? Have all your staff got legal contracts? Are there any contractors that are really employees? Is your incentive scheme or more often your tax effective bonus scheme sustainable to a buyer? It worked for you but will it for them, especially if they are a corporate buyer?

Share structure

Many exits fail because of disparate shareholder requirements. Perhaps it could be an age difference that causes different exit drivers, or possibly simply one needs more money than the other. It is a good idea early on to examine the needs of all parties. It may make sense to purchase a minority share prior to going to market. It could be cheaper and easier. Either way buyers usually require 100% of the share capital.

If a shareholder has more than 25% then they have rights which can effectively veto a sale in the UK. Again this needs looking at early on. Will the minority parties seek to buy the business and undermine the sale process solely with that aim? Generally the best way to deal with different shareholdings is to get everyone to agree on a pro-rata basis. Have dialogue long in advance with all parties. Examine each party's motivations and agree strategies that work for all, and that all shareholders feel they have input into.

Finally, are all the shareholders present and involved? They will all be asked to give warranties to a buyer but will the minority parties be willing to if they are not involved in the business?

Intellectual property

We have already said that IP can create barriers. If you have it why not register it, if not already? If it is registered, are patent renewals up to date?

Litigation

Conclude any litigation, either by or against the company. Such action can seriously damage the goodwill of a business. Buyers may see litigation as the potential tip of an iceberg. One action, they will say, what else has the company done wrong that we will pick up the liability for?

Ownership of tangible/intangible assets

Ensure all assets and intellectual property are properly registered, or licensed to the company.

Review property status

Is your lease or leases due for renewal? Has your unit/s got the right use type on it? Would a buyer seek to relocate your business, will they therefore require flexibility on the lease? Are you paying a commercial rent? If you are a sole trader or Partnership will your lease be assignable? In particular are there any dilapidations on the property that a buyer will be reluctant to take on, or use to reduce the price? Should the freehold be taken out pre-sale?

Environmental

Ensure environmental concerns associated with the business premises, production process or products are understood and minimized. An environmental audit may be appropriate to establish areas of concern. A similar review should be undertaken for the health and safety aspects of the company.

Compliance and legislation

The modern legislative environment is quite stringent, and not just related to employees. Do you comply with all the latest best practice in mailings, data protection, money laundering? EEC regulation needs considering too. Most lawyers will on a 'use me for the deal' basis review this risk and help you tidy up for low or minimal charge. It's not just today's legislation you need to look at: do you need to prepare the business for future legislation? Buyers will prefer companies that have prepared.

Accounts

Profitability

Maximize profitability and reduce non-core business expenditure. Can you increase your gross profit at all? Is it possible to work hard on supplier agreements whilst improving your service and product at the same time, thus being able to increase prices? Are there also expenses that are superfluous? Are there overheads that are just that and they don't generate a return? Could you use IT systems or a different approach to save money? Also, ensure all elements of trading are visible. Buyers hate complicated accounts. It raises too many questions.

Rationalization

Consider separating any part of the business that will not add value to the sale. It may be that you need to hive off a division into a separate company, as it is unlikely to appeal to the same buyer. There could be tax advantages to this. There may also be personal assets in the company that it is worth considering taking out pre-sale. Consider also the most appropriate treatment of loans to the company by yourself.

Balance sheet and accounting standards

Streamline the balance sheet. In particular, review slow moving or obsolete stock, recover aged debts, review the status and value of property or other fixed assets. Do you comply with the current accounting standards?

Taxation

Take advice on the tax considerations, e.g. capital gains tax, reinvestment and rollover relief. Also consider any unused capital allowances particularly where freehold business premises are owned. Both company and personal taxation issues must be considered.

Pre-sale

Information

Ensure information is available and properly recorded to enable a potential acquirer to fully assess the business. This may mean changes to the way information is being recorded and presented.

Advisors

Identify your strategy early on by involving an experienced corporate advisor at the earliest stage.

Tips and techniques for adding value

Focus on adding capital value	Target yourself to add value every day
Always look to improve performance of everything (including after you just improved it)	Go out and get business from day one
Action, action, action. Don't just think, do	Ask customers for their needs, don't rely on guessing what they are
Invest in projects with the highest possible returns	Look for opportunity everywhere
Supply what is needed, not what you want to provide	Leverage your time, money and any other asset
Fast is best. Put speed and efficiency before perfection	Keep it simple
Always look to improve efficiency	Listen
Think long and short-term	Constantly ask, "How can I do what I do for more customers with less work and for a better price?"
Always put money/resources away to see you through a rainy day	Work smart before working harder
Start small, have big idea and break down into manageable chunks	Buy best quality at best price, i.e. best value not lowest price
Don't waste time with every possible customer. Focus your efforts and expertise	Be focused and specialized, one thing at a time
Build long-term repeat customers	Always have your opportunity spectacles on

Do not borrow, unless you really have to; buy what you want when you can	Flash means crash. You don't need the latest furniture, computers, executive cars to run a business
Think, do research before committing to decisions	Take calculated risks and limit/protect the downside
Feel constantly threatened (cash flow, bank, competition, economy, staff…) and prepare ahead of time	Harness your whole concentration upon one goal, achieve it, then move on to the next
Where there is muck there is brass. Often opportunities appear in unpopular areas. Look at the soaring success of Rentokil for example. Look for needs that are not being satisfied	Provide what people want to buy, in the way they want to buy it

Summary

Business owners should plan and prepare for a sale as much in advance as possible. In some cases this preparation may take up to three years, although usually less time is required. Market conditions can also dictate that it may be more profitable to sell now rather then wait and prepare. Preparations to sell, to think about from day one include:

- Having a clear and understandable objective to the sale, as purchasers normally seek justifiable and sensible reasons.
- Obtaining a realistic view of the sale price and deal structure that is likely to be secured (accepting a performance-related payment may need to be considered). Sellers can then decide whether this meets their own objectives.
- Considering the possible buyer and their likely reason for purchase. An understanding of potential purchasers' needs makes it possible to then prepare the business in the best and most advantageous way. This can ease the sale process and make it more profitable.
- Employ a specialist intermediary early on to help you achieve a more profitable sale.

"The fight is won or lost far away from witnesses – behind the lines, in the gym and out there on the road, long before I dance under those lights."

Muhammad Ali

REALITY CHEQUE

MARINE PUBLISHER
S. EAST

T/O £480,000 **MARCH 2003**

For Astrid Powell running her own business was the perfect way to combine earning a living and raising her young child. After fifteen years working as the European sales representative of a large US-based marine publication, Astrid made the bold decision to approach and buy her UK competitor. Although it was a gamble she knew that she had the expertise to make the business succeed and that she could run her business from home, fitting her working hours in with the demands of motherhood.

Astrid owned and published a business-to-business magazine, predominately read by professional designers and engineers within a niche sector of the marine industry. With a worldwide circulation of almost 12,000 the majority of which was outside Europe, the magazine's approach under Astrid's leadership was lively and punchy, ensuring a loyal readership and high levels of reader response.

With a small staff of five, including Astrid, who ran the business on a day-to-day basis, she developed the brand and launched an excellent, interactive web site to support the magazine. As the business grew so did the responsibilities and Astrid's workload. In addition, due to personal reasons, Astrid's editor had to resign and she found herself taking on increasing amounts of the editorial work. She found herself working late into the night and over the weekend, and eventually the burden of work became too much.

She realized that the time had come to sell the business and approached Avondale. After careful research into the sector Avondale approached a number of specialist publishers. Within three months of marketing the business two potential purchasers had had meetings with Astrid and one made an offer which provided the perfect solution for Astrid.

The purchaser owned a group of marine publications and already had the resources to run Astrid's magazine and further develop it whilst making a number of economies of scale. The deal gave Astrid the majority of the consideration on completion with a small amount deferred over the next year. However, the most attractive part of the deal was that the purchaser was keen to retain Astrid on a full-time basis.

Nine months after completion Astrid is doing what she has always enjoyed, working on the sales and marketing side of the magazine, with an input into the future of the publication but with none of the worries and responsibilities of owning the business. And the icing on the cake is that the purchaser's office is only ten minutes away from her front door! As Astrid herself says, "It is the perfect deal!"

"Continuous effort – not strength or intelligence – is the key to unlocking our potential."

Sir Winston Churchill

chapter eight Branding – The difference that makes the difference

EIGHT Branding – The difference that makes the difference

"We must either find a way or make one."
Hannibal

"The best preparation for good work tomorrow is to do good work today."
Elbert Hubbard

"Being good in business is the most fascinating kind of art."
Andy Warhol

Chapter focus

Continuing from the last chapter we look at a key component of adding value, branding. A good brand creates customer loyalty, enhances profits and therefore increases the value of your business in the eyes of potential eventual buyers. In this chapter we cover how to make your company stand out and thus increase your sales price. A lot of the areas we cover come under marketing skills. This is a very involved, detailed and psychological area of business management so we attempt, we hope, to give insight at the foundations, rather than look at the hundreds of ways businesses can market or brand themselves.

- **Introduction**
- **Examples of branding success**
- **Managing the brand**
- **Vive la difference!**
- **Invent a niche and market**
- **Listening**

Introduction

Most professional advice on increasing the value of your business will be from financial people and thus will tend to focus on the financials of a business. However, we believe that this ignores the true heart of a business, the marketing function. Yes, of course the financials are important and have a significant bearing on your valuation, but people do not always buy on cost. In fact, marketing studies show that most people buy on emotion. They buy from people they like, or brands they are familiar with, or recommendation. Cost has an impact but how can anyone therefore justify a Ferrari? It is impractical on today's roads, fuel inefficient and very expensive, and yet most dream of owning one. Why? It is exactly that – the dream and all the associations that come with it. It is the same with a company sale. To achieve the best sale price your business needs to connect on a positive emotional level with both your customers and potential buyers. To achieve this we believe you need to 'manage the brand' carefully.

A brand is an identity for your company and what it provides, particularly in terms of quality and service. To be useful the brand should stand out and should generate positive associations with your customers. Once a brand is established it greatly encourages customers to return and recommend your services to others. The reliability and consistency of the brand takes out the unknown and helps customers to make a purchase decision. It makes us repeat customers, and repeat customers increase profits, value and saleability. Just think in valuing the McDonalds Empire how much those golden arches are worth!

To get a customer the first time is hard work. Getting the same ones back will strengthen your business. It therefore makes sense, depending on your business, to keep him or her for the long-term and set him or her up as someone that would recommend you. Surveys show it is 5 times more expensive to procure a new customer than it is to retain a loyal customer. Brand generates this loyalty, and it can be managed.

Interestingly, the accounting definition of the valuation of goodwill is the difference between the price paid and the company's net asset value. Yet, the word goodwill if you look it up means a feeling of benevolence, of trust of wellbeing to someone or something. Goodwill can therefore be measured by how much trust your customers have in your business. Typically, the higher this trust, the stronger the profits and growth prospects of the business and therefore its value. Your brand has a huge bearing on the trust that customers place in your business and therefore it significantly affects the value of your business.

Examples of branding success

Whatever industry we look at there are the flash-in-the-pans that have their moment of glory, but never grow beyond a small business. Then there are those that lead and develop. Even in the music industry there are hosts of stars on every radio station never to be heard of again a year later. And then there are those like Madonna that keep producing stuff and stay at the top. What makes a big long-term success? What enables them to lead and then keep leading? This is what a buyer of your business will pay a premium for. The International Virgin brand for example suggests fun, value and sense of spirit, which translates well into a business formula. A motor executive once said to me that when someone pays over £20,000 for a car, they are paying at least £5,000 for the 50p badge on the front!

Imagine a situation where buyers look at four companies of similar size and industry to yours. What criteria do you think they will use to decide upon the one they acquire? What criterion would you use? What made any company the leader in its field: McDonalds, Marks & Spencers, Amazon, Microsoft, Disney, Virgin? All of these companies differentiated themselves from their competitors. It is this sparkle of difference and being special that investors look for. It shows potential for development.

Business is not necessarily about having the best products or the best prices. It is not about logic. People don't buy on price as much is as commonly thought. In fact they may prefer a high price to a lower one.

Managing the brand

In our experience many small business owners tend to think of a brand as their corporate trademark or product benefit, but it is much greater than that. To name a few, brand management encompasses managing the following disciplines: PR, events management, company vision and culture, product focus, logos, statements, price promises, training, trademarks and recruitment approach. Indeed, we liken brand management to managing the personality of the company and, as we all know, personalities can be intensely complicated. However, if you think of the brand as a person, it makes sense. Obviously image and look contribute to a person's success, but their values, belief system, attitude, motivation and vision are just as likely to determine the person's success. So it is with a company.

When you think of a brand like a person you can also see other benefits. People generally know and stick to what they are good at. Again this is the same with companies. Brands do of course cross barriers into new sectors, however a brand known for value would probably be making a mistake diversifying into premium products. Another thought, people get preconceptions about other people pretty immediately in a relationship and these are hard to change. It is again the same with companies. For example, if your company can generate the preconception that it offers exclusivity, it does not matter whether in fact it necessarily does all the time. Or, if the exclusive brand diversifies into a new area, the new product may be presumed to be exclusive simply by association. In recent years there have been more BMW 3 series on the UK roads than Ford Mondeos, yet it is still felt they retain their exclusive nature, but how? The company works hard at a prestige image and the price tag is hardly common. It is an emotional thing, not necessarily logical.

To the consumer a brand represents an intrinsic value proposition, which enables them to choose probably emotionally one particular brand over another. Considering the following questions should help you understand your brand more closely:

- What business is our brand **really** in?
- What differentiates our products and services from our competitors?
- What is superior about the value we offer our customers?
- How do customers see us and how do we want to be seen?

What business is our brand in? This is perhaps the most important and, on the surface, simplest question. However, it is not simple. There are many companies that have gone bust as a result of not having the right answer to this question. In the UK only 5 of the top 100 FTSE listed companies were there 20 years ago. This means new contenders and brands have come and replaced the old ones. How? Often, we believe it as a result of the old not understanding this question, and the new understanding it.

The best-known example has to be IBM. In the '70s, you see, they thought their business and brand was that of developing and selling the best computer mainframes to companies. What they missed was the PC revolution. Had their brand simply been providing systems of any type to help people, business or otherwise, they might well have developed and owned the PC market. Instead the crown has gone to others. Wang, who benefited from the short-sightedness of major typewriter companies to become the world's leading word processing company, also fell victim to the PC. Had Wang and the typewriter companies understood their business was allowing people to communicate through the written word they may have done things differently, and instead of disappearing again owned a major part of the PC global business. They might even have won the Internet, after all the email is (to date) the ultimate global written communication. Imagine that – a typewriter company developing the Internet.

So the key is not what your product or company does, but what it enables people to do on a big picture level that is important. It is your customers' dream requirement that your brand is delivering. Ferrari does not deliver a car; it delivers a dream lifestyle of exotic beaches, performance, fast living, wealth and success.

It is the dream that your brand is delivering. For example, a garage might think their business is repairing and servicing cars. In reality the driving experience is much more than that. It's about keeping people mobile and creating convenience. A garage that recognizes this might start marketing itself differently. Certainly the inconvenience of being without a car during the service is a key area to focus on so hence we might start looking at free drop offs or collection, courtesy vehicles or taxi returns as a means of creating client convenience. A garage that becomes known for caring about customers' convenience is beginning to develop a way of doing things and a positive reputation as a result.

The brand is now developing. Now the garage needs to bring the concept into the signage, strap-lines, advertising and procedures. Further changes might be made. For example, staff training might be undertaken about what inconveniences customers and how best to avoid these things. A transparent pricing procedure might be adopted stating that all jobs will be pre-priced and the reason for them pre-explained. This would mean that even if the customer were facing bad news he or she would receive no nasty shocks, uncertainties and inconvenience as a result.

As the garage becomes more sophisticated and the team gets the idea, it may be possible to get the mechanics to suggest ways of removing inconvenience. In other words it is the owners job to perhaps establish the concept, but they don't have to come up with all the ideas. Indeed, it is preferable if they do not. If the team helps build and have 'ownership' of the brand you have the most powerful formula for growth. Okay, this is pretty basic and we are not qualified to run a garage but, hopefully, the example helps you get an idea of what we mean by brand management.

What differentiates us? The second and third questions are also interesting. We all hear the marketing term unique selling points (USPs) used, but what do they really mean? Many companies brand themselves on selling points without considering the differential; that is what makes them unique. Many selling points are simply hygiene points anyway. For example, hygiene in a restaurant or exceptional customer service is surely something we should all expect and that companies should have in any case. How can it be a USP?

Relevant differentiation is the key. To create a brand, we have to set our brand apart from everyone else in the market. It is almost impossible to build a brand by being the same. The differentiation also has to be meaningful and therefore enable customers to place the company, product or service at a higher esteem than others available. The differentiation should create a perceived or real value to customers, which enables them to prefer and choose it.

How do customers see us and how do we want to be seen? The fourth question is often the most difficult. You see, knowing what business you are really in and achieving relevant differentiation are not enough. An effective medium has to be chosen to communicate the dream and difference, and enable the customer to understand and believe it. It is not enough for a company to say, "We have a dream" or relevant differentiation. It has to be heard, understood and believed externally. Communication is not what you say or how you say it, but what is heard. What the customer hears ultimately dictates where your brand stands now, and why they care or perhaps sometimes don't care about your company, product or service.

It helps again to think of the brand as a person. Imagine if someone says they are going to do something but never does it. What is your perception of that person? It is that they never deliver what they say they will. Thus again it is with companies. If a company offers a price promise or service level, it damages the trust it has with the customer if it does not deliver. In our opinion therefore, doing what you say you will and by when, is a vital part of brand management.

Once a message (dream and differentiator) has been identified it must be framed in a succinct message that people (staff and clients) can understand and relate to. Then it must be repeated and repeated and repeated. This will reinforce the message and core value of the product and service.

Make sure the brand is reflected in your whole approach. We reckon this is so important it may even, for true brand managers, have a bearing on your personnel. If, for example, as a professional practice you pride yourself on best advice and being objective (doing the right thing even if it is not in your interest), do you really want selfish self-centred people on the team? The danger is that they may well undermine your brand, by acting the opposite to it. Be the message. There must be a direct connection between your brand message and your customers' experience. Every single member of your team must understand and agree with the brand and its values.

The rules of brand management

1. Think of your brand as an identity. It has a personality that needs to be managed.
2. Focus on what your company enables people to do, not what you do (the dream).
3. Position the brand by defining where you are in the market and what type of customer should want to use you.
4. Choose relevant differentiators, not hygiene (expected to have) points.
5. Communicate the relevant differences effectively at every step and level, throughout the organization and to customers. In that order: many businesses tell their customers but forget to tell their staff.
6. Develop an image, logo and strap-line that communicate your dream and differentiator.
7. Align your businesses, procedures, training, recruitment, PR and approach around what your business really does and why it is so different.
8. Ensure you never undermine your brand. It must be spoken about and believed at every level.

Vive la difference!

There are many ways to be different, for example:

- Speedier service (Eurodrive, Amazon, FedEx)
- More quality (Stella Artois, Harrods, Cadbury's)
- More value for money (Halifax, Burger King)
- Cheap, no frills (Easy Jet, Asda)
- More choice, more value (Tesco)
- Delivered or packaged in a unique way (Argos)
- Fun (Virgin)
- Better warranties (Rover)
- Guaranteed results (Parcel World)
- No fuss replacement policy (Marks & Spencer, Argos)
- Available for business at certain locations or times
- Free trial (AOL, Which magazine)
- Size (Monster.com)
- Safety (Volvo)
- Driving machine (BMW)
- Build quality (Mercedes)
- Most supported product (Microsoft)
- Creative, always new things (Disney)
- Prestige in ownership (Rolls Royce, Rolex)
- Prestige in shopping there (Harrods, Selfridges)
- Environmentally friendly (The Body Shop)
- Mature (Saga Holidays)
- Young (18-30 Holidays)

There are many more, and we have put companies we associate with those differences. Are we right? Would the companies be pleased or displeased by our associations? Difference for the sake of it will not make you rich. It is when that difference matches a need in a sector of the buying market. Your branding needs to say, "This product is unique, better, what you need and reflects who you are."

We suggest you become obsessed with meeting changing consumer needs. Be wary of working for your needs, you must keep your focus on the customer. You may like and believe in something passionately or really want to do something a certain way, but does anybody with money to spend agree with you? New entrepreneurs are so often caught up in the genius of their own ideas that they forget to be a good listener. Research, research and listen.

In building your business, it will be easier if every customer you win stays with you long-term. This loyalty comes through the branding experience. Whereas the branding image you settle on comes from outside of the company, it needs to be identified with internally in the company. They will then capitalize on it and identify with it, and feel they are a class above the competitors. This will have the effect of encouraging loyalty from customers and staff.

- We don't buy vacuum cleaners, we buy Hoovers
- We don't buy ballpoint pens, we buy Biros
- We don't buy burgers, we go to McDonalds
- We don't go for a coffee, we meet at Starbucks

To build up a brand, like many things in business, requires long-term thinking. The work is this month but the rewards are rarely this month. You have to develop the total customer experience into an image for your company. The logo, strap lines etc. just reflect the image that represents a set of values, service and satisfaction. Marks & Spencer's in the UK and Europe built a reputation for quality. Both of us can remember our respective parents being loyal to Marks due to their quality and no fuss returns policy. A policy like that does not have a short-term gain, but such branding led them to becoming a household name on the retail scene.

The ideal is to build your brand to the point where your customers recommend you by word of mouth. Recommendation is totally free advertising; you don't have to pay a commission for it. Imagine an advertisement in the paper for a new restaurant's impact compared to a friend recommending a restaurant. Which one would you go to?

Give consumers a reason to buy into your branding and merge it with their personal identity. Like fashion houses that print their names on the outside of clothes so that customers can show the world; Yves St Laurent and Gucci are examples.

A brand can evolve to keep in tune with market moves. The fast food industry has many clear brands with its many franchised outlets McDonalds, Kentucky Fried Chicken, etc. However people are increasingly putting healthy eating higher up their list of criteria. Thus these companies have the challenge of moving with these trends. There are signs that they are doing this now, testing out the appeal of new products. The instantly recognizable brand means we know what we are going to get wherever we may be in the world. The question is, is this still what we really want? Perhaps we are all still going into these outlets for lack of an alternative that one day could take this market by storm.

The motor industry offers clear brands and is an excellent field to study for ideas. Whatever the car, they all basically do the same job, and yet there is tremendous divergence and branding differences in what we choose even within a particular price bracket. As cars have all broadly got better the main difference between manufacturers is today how they market and differentiate themselves through their branding. In many cases their product development follows the brand rather than the other way around.

Invent a niche and market

Good marketing is about the profitable satisfaction of customers' needs. Most companies start off with a sales orientation. They don't worry so much about profit or customer needs; they are just keen to sell goods. However, long-term this is a limited strategy. It does nothing to retain customers or create loyalty. It may not even be profitable as margin is often lost to shift volume. As the business matures, the wise business owner switches from a sales orientation to a marketing orientation. This means they stop worrying so much about volume but start thinking about quality, building margins (remember, people rarely buy just on price) and the experience the customer achieves.

Sometimes in this transition an odd phenomenon occurs. The business often needs to take a step backwards in order to gain forward, but why?

Essentially it is because to become marketing orientated you need to define your customer better in order to build passionate loyalty from perhaps fewer, rather than broad indifference from many. Aiming at a niche customer profile seems brave but it is vital. Imagine a 27 year old on a Saga mature persons' holiday, or a 65 year old on a Club 18-30 young persons' holiday. They don't mix and the marketing has to say so otherwise neither will go. You narrow your focus, products or service (or loose some) in order to say to the customer this is what we are good at, this is what we specialize in and we want you. We call this becoming niche.

Surprisingly perhaps, if you define an audience as niche you often get a broader audience as a result. Surf fashion shops, for example, appeal to people who can't surf but love the carefree beach appeal of the goods. Better still, by focusing on just surfers, the shop can create a distinctive image that stands out, and possibly charge a premium for its goods over other shops as a result.

In an ideal world, rather than starting a business and then developing into a new niche, it would be better to start in a niche in the first place. However, this requires very careful market research or bravery, as you don't know what a customer wants. Ideally you will be the first to find a niche, as history tells us the first (as long as they are fast) to a market ends up ahead. Microsoft being the first in the PC market is a classic example, or Henry Ford first with the affordable mass-produced motor car.

If you conclude that your chances of being first in a sector are slim, then the answer might be to redefine the sector you are in, within the overall market, thus creating a niche that you are recognized for and own. You then develop a brand that is recognized for doing something. Dyson clearly did this with the market for vacuum cleaners, winning in a market against Hoover, where the market leader's brand was so strong their company name entered the dictionary for the products they made.

Example of entrepreneurs who successfully reinvented their sector:

- Stelios Haji – Ioannou – Easy Jet. Not everyone flies business class.
- Bill Gates – Microsoft. Personal computing
- Jeff Bezo – Amazon. Books on-line
- James Dyson. People would buy a vacuum cleaner that did not have a bag that kept clogging with dust

- Martha Lane Fox – lastminute.com. People do a range of things at the last minute
- Richard Branson – Virgin Group. His personality as a brand makes his companies stand out to customers (beware though of this approach as it ties you into the business)
- Fred Smith – Fed Ex. 'Overnight' global courier.

If you have not got an original idea, take one from somebody or somewhere else. There are many entrepreneurs who have visited other countries, noticed something different that has worked and brought it home. Jack Cohen was a London market trader originally who then opened stores. He went to the USA and saw self-service in operation, which was radical at the time. He came back to the UK, introduced it in his shops and his fortune zoomed. Those who shop at Tesco in the UK (and Europe today) will know just how far he progressed. These days with the Internet you can find out what is happening in the States without even leaving home. Jack Cohen incidentally is a good example of someone working in and on his business. He developed these new innovations but he could still reputedly tell you what was in a can without a label by shaking it!

Look at successful companies all around you and you will notice that they did something different to their competitors that made them stand out and progress faster. Often you will find taking ideas from different industries is easier than from your own. By definition usually anything you learn from your own industry somebody is already doing. There are various ways to differentiate your company. To name a few:

- Efficiency in operations
- Customer service
- Originality
- Best value for money
- Cheapest
- Highest quality
- New distribution methodology
- Location
- Product

- Contract
- Personnel
- Training
- Branding
- Trade names, patents, copyright

Think of things that you have bought in the last month. Or perhaps visit your kitchen and open the fridge. What car do you drive? Where do you go shopping? Whose clothes do you wear? What brands are you buying and why? How did they influence you? And what can you apply to your own business from these thoughts?

Invent a sector, or find a niche. Focus on it, promote it, market it, repeat it and re-promote it. The most valuable company in any given sector is the market leader or the threat to it.

Listening

Be careful of being carried away and wrapped up in your dream. Glossy brochures, attractive web sites, plush office furniture are usually justified as marketing spend, image, something like that, but they are only part of the whole customer experience.

Branding is not synonymous with marketing spend. The customer has a different set of needs that rarely include a glossy brochure or web site. They are often there for the entrepreneur's vanity. All of these things boil down to statements that say, "Why we are so fantastic". Your energies would be better invested getting other people, ideally past customers to say that you are fantastic. Entrepreneurs are out there selling their dream, the thing they have a passion for which tends to create more talking than listening. This tends to mean that they are not naturally good listeners. It is through listening though that the market will tell you what it wants to buy, particularly what is missing right now.

The best way to find out how your customers perceive your business is to ask them. Conduct a short, simple survey of a sample and see what they say. You may be surprised. You will probably be given clues as to how you can improve your service, niches that you can move into etc. You should conduct such a survey in our opinion on a regular basis. Why did your current customers buy from you? Who are they and what are they doing? Who looks like they are positioned to move ahead and why? What can you offer that they cannot? What can you do better?

Listening is vital, although a word of caution. The customer is not always right and they don't know always what they are telling you, or what they want. Xerox asked their customers if they wanted the photocopier and the reply was a resounding 'no'. People did not understand the benefits. Fortunately for us Xerox did and they pushed ahead with their plans anyway.

Summary

The business which generates positive emotion in its customers with a strong margin and a way of doing things, is likely to be the most successful and therefore the most valuable. Brands are like people. The more they stand out the more we like them. If you can own a niche, product, customer charter or way of doing things that is different, logical in the sector and hard to replace you will make yourself the most valuable business in any given sector. If your business gives acquirers a 'we want/we need' motivation it will increase the premium they are willing to pay for it. Apart from anything else a strong brand will increase the number or buyers for your business, and, as we have just in part examined in this chapter, rare popular items always sell for more.

"In order to be irreplaceable one must always be different."

Coco Chanel

chapter nine Leader/managers – Showing the way

NINE Leader/managers – Showing the way

"A manager is not a person who can do the work better than his men; he is a person who can get his men to do the work better than he can."

Fred Smith (Federal Express)

"If you do things well, do them better. Be daring, be first, be different, be just."

Anita Roddick

Chapter focus

This chapter takes a practical look at the role of leader in the small growth firm and how to balance this with day-to-day management.

- **Introduction**
- **Leader management invest in and retain people**
- **Motivating people**
- **Build a community (culture)**
- **Leader/managers in the real world**
- **Warning signs of when leadership is lacking**
- **Leadership on purchase**
- **Leadership succession**
- **Summary**

Introduction

Good leadership and management produce synergy, energy, enthusiasm and hard focused work. These are key aspects required to grow a business in order to make it profitable and the most valuable if a sale exit is eventually sought. In a small firm you have limited resources and therefore you need the leverage, power and productivity of a strong co-ordinated team. They need to work together consistently, at full power, and towards clear goals, even when the management is not there. So long as it is a productive team, as a general rule of thumb the bigger and more successful the team, the bigger, more profitable and valuable the business. This means that staff are not an overhead, they are an asset and employing, motivating and developing a team is a large and essential part of building a successful business venture.

This chapter is a short checklist on leadership and, in part, management. Particular attention is paid to the principles of leadership in small to medium-sized firms. In addition, at the end of the chapter we explore several succession issues for the entrepreneur and the various requirements of new managers and their approach to staff on completion of an acquisition. Human resource is far more of a challenge to management than financial or technical resource so we concentrate on this area. Businesses are run and carried out by people, for people.

Leader/managers

How much leadership influences success in a business is hard to quantify, particularly in many larger, already successful businesses. In smaller firms however, the management and their approach determines success or failure, no matter how good the business concept.

People often confuse management with leadership; managers are organizers and leaders are inspirers. In most small to medium-sized businesses the owner/entrepreneurs have the role of both. Interestingly and perhaps understandably, many are good at one aspect and not the other. The most successful businesses (profitable and valuable on sale) are, in our experience, run by leader/managers. These are people who combine excellence in organization and inspiration. Where they are weak they employ the right team to provide this combination. Leader management, like other business skills, can be learned and applied through practice. There are many different styles and most people will be good at some aspects and not others. The key is to play on your strengths and work on your weaknesses.

Below we have compiled the key rules of leader management as we see them. Break the rules at your peril.

Rule 1 – *Have a clear vision*

Have a clear ambitious and profitable vision of where you are going to take the business. Even if you have doubts, it is enough to choose a clear destination. Don't expect everyone to share your vision (theirs might be taking the kids to Disneyland). Your vision should be one that people are prepared to follow and drive at. It is a bonus if they share it. Our experience suggests that the best way to achieve this is to get people involved in choosing and building the vision from an early stage.

Break the destination down into individual goals that make up the whole. Make the goals stretching (each one progressively harder) rather than aiming for the stars at each step. Then motivate and help people to achieve goals. Put your vision in writing and share it from top to bottom in the organization. This creates clarity and removes inconsistencies, shortfalls and problems. It also helps people give you advice on your plan.

Some examples of vision include:

Bill Gates	To put a PC in every person's home in the world.
Jeff Bezos (Amazon)	Building a place where people can come and find and discover anything they want to buy online.
James Dyson	Putting research and technology back into making products that the world wants.
Anita Roddick (Body Shop)	Profits with principles

Rule 2 – *Be flexible*

Embrace and seek change. Just because something has always been done one way it does not mean it is the right or best way. What was best once may be no longer, due to other changes. If something is not working alter it, always with the goal and vision in mind.

Rule 3 – *Listen and react*

Listen to your staff, your customers and your market. Take the time to stay in touch and understand their needs and what is happening in the business, and therefore what needs to be done. It is important to delegate but avoid ivory tower syndrome (being too distant to understand what is really happening). Step back and look at the overall picture and then work on the shop floor from time to time. Then react to change, opportunities and threats. Some of the most successful leader/managers we know are still sales/dealmakers. Although this can cause problems with a sale as the business can have a dependency on them, it is an excellent way of staying in touch and delivering income at the same time. If this approach is used, plan how to step away prior to a sale.

Don't always invest in what you have always invested in. Just because you and the business used to do something a certain way does not mean it is right now. Are there other ways to do it?

Rule 4 – *Be tough and responsible*

You have to be reasonably tough to run your own business. People look for and expect the leader to have courage and strength to get them through the ups and downs of commercial life and secure their jobs. Their strength is drawn from their leader. This does not mean you can't talk about or share problems. A fool thinks he is wise, a wise man thinks he is a fool. Draw confidence from accepting you can't know everything, nor be right all the time.

True leaders also accept ultimate responsibility. They know if it has gone wrong, they must learn from this. Yes, external factors have an impact, but then perhaps more could be done next time. Being tough means you can deal with and learn from failure, and are also prepared to bear responsibility.

Rule 5 – *Choose conflict over harmony*

There are times when difficult things have to be said. Don't avoid saying them. If one of your team is struggling or has missed the point it is far better to tell it how it is. Do so in a tactful, constructive, planned, non-personal and objective way. Give examples and support to work past the situation. Likewise, if tough decisions have to be made, make them. Business is about survival. Do not confuse being tough with not caring. This is a similar principle to tough love. Sometimes you have to be cruel to be kind.

Rule 6 – *Be decisive*

Business moves in real time and thus you need to be quick, not always having the time you would like to make decisions. You need to have strong convictions followed by equally strong actions. Balance this with as much foresight, planning and research as possible. Manage the potential downsides and risks. A poor decision implemented well through good organization and change management will generally be more successful than a bad one implemented poorly.

Rule 7 – *Be disciplined and organized*

You have no immediate direct boss to give you orders, listen to your frustrations and support you with your problems. You are alone and must therefore have self control and be organized. This means setting yourself rules and goals and sticking to them. The same applies for your business. Leading a small business is about exploiting good ideas, being practical about their implementation to deadline and refining and tweaking them.

Rule 8 – *Inspire*

Everything that we do has a motive. Our actions are the visible results of drives, although these are often divergent. For example, if in the short-term the pleasure of chocolate is stronger than the long-term goal of being thin, then you will eat chocolate. So don't think that you have to teach motivation, it is there naturally in abundance. It is the direction and focus of it that you have to work on. You cannot actually motivate people, only set the groundwork for them to motivate themselves. Approaches include:

- Listen
- Encourage self esteem
- Recognize success and say thank you
- Set and encourage challenges
- Dramatize ideas
- Take the time to understand your teams own personal vision/goals
- Embrace failures as learning exercises (the first time only though!)
- Get people involved and give them ownership of goals
- Infuse thought, ideas, feeling and passion; it's infectious.

Most people will be happy feeling part of a team and having satisfying work to do and to know they are making a valuable contribution. You also need to be aware that quite often individuals do not have the same clarity on their personal career goals as you must have on the goals for the enterprise. When people believe in themselves there is no stopping them.

Rule 9 – *Be noble*

People need to know where they stand. This means you need a consistent personal code of conduct. If you are dishonest, unfair or ruthless you will surround yourself with either the weak or those that have the same attributes; neither is good for the business. We suggest that a noble approach is best. Here are a few tips:

Honesty is the best policy	Take time to understand others and their personal vision goals
Never lie (if you can't answer, say so)	Be fair but don't confuse this with being soft
Keep it simple	Admit your mistakes
Be magnanimous (avoid politics and pettiness)	Always do what you say you are going to do
Listen to ideas	Tell it how it is
Never steal ideas from your team (always thank them)	Say thank you!
Respect others views even if you disagree	

Rule 10 – *Seek clarity*

There is an old joke about World War One that the General sent a message, "Send reinforcements, we are going to advance." By the time this reached HQ it had become, "Send three and four pence, we are gong to a dance!" Take responsibility for your message getting through in the way you intended it. If your staff misinterprets you, it is your fault for not communicating clearly. If you find saying things like, "I have told you this time and time again and you're still doing it wrong", then you need to work on your communication skills, not they on theirs.

Rule 11 – *Delegate*

Most people want and feel proud of responsibility, so give it to them. Be aware of people's capabilities, and provide training and tools for support where necessary. Show interest and encouragement in delegated tasks. The ultimate leader/manager is one who puts them out of a job by having a team machine that functions on a day-to-day basis without them. Better still, one who gets his/her team to drive them and the business rather than the other way around. Here are just a few delegating tips:

- Create clear lines of responsibility, job roles and ownership of responsibility
- Set clear goals with your team and don't rest until they are achieved
- Involve your team in these goals
- Get your team to set realistic deadlines on themselves
- Create a feedback process. Reports/reports and reports. Keep notes
- Get it in writing
- Check, support and encourage progress
- Reward and recognizes success
- Avoid upwards delegation. If there is a problem, don't immediately solve it; ask them for the solution first
- Let go of what you can, but remember it is still your responsibility to track the job and make sure it is done
- Work on the business, not in it.

Sometimes it takes more time to delegate a task than to do it however, remember, once a task has been successfully delegated it can be repeated time and time again. This buys more time for the manager on other tasks. Take pride in achieving through others. You don't need acknowledgement, they do. Encourage, nurture and be proud of your team's success and progress.

Rule 12 – *Be informed*

Knowledge is power. The more you know and hear the more you can apply. Leader/managers are constantly seeking new ideas, developments and inspirations. These can come from staff, competitors, other business practices, websites, books, networking organizations, seminars, trade associations, holidays to different business environments and conversations. Set up a realistic plan of continuous input from external sources and stick to it. A typical plan might include:

Monthly	Bi-monthly	6 months
Attend one seminar	Read a book	Brainstorm with team for ideas
Find and circulate one useful website	Attend a trade meeting	Set vision update/workshop progress
Read various trade and business press	Target and research one competitor and their approach	Travel for pleasure and look. How do they do it elsewhere in the world? (Yes, you get a holiday too!)
Note: You may be able to delegate some of the above but ask for key updates.		

Rule 13 – *Encourage innovation*

A good idea can add more to your business than a free loan from the bank. Six brains are six times more likely to come up with a good idea than one, especially if they are inspiring each other. Therefore your leadership needs to encourage and reward the flow of ideas. It also needs to accept that with ideas can come failure, so seeing failure as part of learning is also essential.

- Encourage brainstorming
- Ask what, if or how can we make it better every day
- Seek suggestions and give feedback even if the idea can't be implemented with clear reasons why
- Listen to and recognize ideas (never steal them, well, from your team at least!)
- Market research. Regularly get competitors' literature, join trade organizations, go to workshops and seminars, research the web, read business books, network. Be a sponge for information on what is going on.

Rule 14 – *Be yourself*

Applying the rules does not mean you have to forget who you are. All good leader/managers have their own style and eccentricities. Indeed, there is a saying: before you presume to lead others, know who you are. Follow your own heart and don't try to be somebody you are not. It is a good idea to take on a role model but make sure it's someone you can relate to. Many female leaders try and take on the archetypal male role model (strong, competitive and hard) so they can manage the male team. They then struggle, as often this can suppress their natural style, which might be a more nurture style approach. Anita Roddick, who founded the Body Shop, is a shining example of a marvellous company built upon clearly female values and style.

Rule 15 – *Build an efficient machine*

Imagine your business is a production line. Design a system, set procedures, get reports, use technology and seek efficiencies. Create clear job roles, ownership of responsibilities and procedures. Back them up with training and accountability.

Once established constantly look for efficiencies and improvements. Kaizen is the Japanese principle of constant change. It purports that every component of a business can and must be improved. Even if the improvement is 10% here, 10% there, soon you have 100% improvement. However efficient you are, you can always be more efficient.

Rule 16 – *Invest in productivity and people*

It is not actions that count, its results. Look at your resources. How can you invest in them to increase productivity? Often because money is tight in smaller ventures the decision of what resources to have is currently cost-led. This means that today's cheap option is often opted for. Occasionally this is right, however the key is to look for resources that are cost-effective, not cost-led. Cheap can be expensive. Go for the best you can afford, but work smart by looking at the price earnings ratio whenever you invest anywhere, i.e. the upfront cost versus the future income stream.

Ask every day on every component:

- How can we increase productivity?
- Is the return on our investment acceptable?
- Can the return we generate be increased?
- Time is money – how can we save time?

Invest in and retain people

One of our rules is to invest in productivity. This requires investment in people. Many see this as paying higher salaries and increasing the training bill. We have already seen however, that money is not the primary motivator of most people, and therefore if this approach is taken in isolation, it is not enough. Failure to invest in people is very expensive.

A high staff turnover means:

- An expensive payroll as you are forced to buy the right people to join you
- A waste of management time recruiting
- A costly training and recruitment bill
- A drain where your organization's tacit knowledge is constantly flushed. Probably the biggest cost.

In contrast to the annual accounts, many companies have plaques on their reception walls saying that their staff are their greatest asset. If you recruited Richard Branson to be your Non-Executive Marketing Director, do you think that would increase the value of your firm? Well, he would not be listed in the balance sheet. The PC that you gave him would be though! Key people are free to resign at any time and thus how can they be assets if you can lose them so easily? You cannot sell them after all. Our view is that if accountants did have a formula for valuing key staff in the balance sheet, managers would spend more attention to keeping staff turnover lower.

Motivating people

Even leader/managers who know the rules will struggle to keep loyalty unless they understand the people that make up their organization today, or those they will need in the future. This requires an understanding of people's motivations, which in itself is a subject that psychologists spend life-times researching. There are nevertheless some basics.

People have both long-term and short-term motivation. Survival is their first instinct. In a capitalist society money (salary/package) is therefore crucial. Having said that, once survival (roof/food/warmth) is achieved, it starts to decrease as a motivating factor. Self-esteem and self-actualization replace them. In other words most people are motivated by their self-development through contribution, value, relationships and health. In order to find long-term motivations you need to find your teams and the individuals, and match these to the business. Don't assume that people will instantly be motivated to be lazy. Actually, so long as they are doing something worthwhile most people enjoy work.

Even a motivated team with long-term goals and motivations will have bad days. The leader/manager's role is to look for short-term fixes to these, whether it be buying them lunch or just stopping and listening.

The leader/manager approach should, by its nature, motivate your team, but there are other tools available. Once you understand the team, careful time and thought should be given to which tools to use. To name a few there are staff days, flexi-working, dress down days, thank you bonuses, pensions, share issues (for long-term wealth), salary increases, recognition awards and cars. By far the most important remains caring about your team's success and making sure it is in balance to the business. There are many ways to demotivate. Driving a Ferrari to the office, not contributing, not respecting nor listening to a team who you deliberately keep underpaid in order to have the Ferrari is probably the ultimate sin. Oh, and not saying thank you for good work.

One company we know takes their whole team of 70 people on a skiing holiday every year. The accountants think they are crazy. However their staff turnover is far lower than the norm for their industry, reducing significantly their recruitment and training bill. It also ensures that knowledge is retained in the business. In other words it's a cost effective investment. It also provides an opportunity for the staff to really get to know each other and develop a team identity and culture. This sparks off ideas, innovation and better cross-department communication.

Build a community (culture)

Probably the most powerful way long-term to motivate and retain people is to give them a sense of belonging. If people feel proud of being part of an organization and they relate to it they will stay and be motivated to make it better.

Work (an application of effort to a purpose) is often seen as a negative requirement in our lives. After all we would rather be at play. Here lies the problem. Most people separate work and play. This is probably because historically they have been made (negative) to work, and they have chosen (positive) to play. The key therefore for the leader/manager is to design an organization or, to put it another way, a community where people enjoy their work, want to do it and they see it as fun, satisfying and purposeful.

Imagine yourself as a newly elected small town mayor. Your job is to make the community (your business) relaxed, interesting, flexible, productive, proud and hard working. A town place where people want to move and live in the long-term. One that they want to contribute to and improve, that they believe in and that will win awards. If your town is to win awards you have to have a vision for that town and a consensus of the town and what the people want. After all, you can't dictate to people to make improvements or force them to live somewhere. If we stick with our example the first step for the mayor would be to call a meeting and ask the townsfolk how they feel about things. What makes the town a good place, what would make it a better place, or what is it they really don't like about it.

Working through consensus the Mayor (a patient person) would agree with the townsfolk what the town stands for, and what the people want it to stand for. This could be summarized into a simple statement. Perhaps it might be 'Sunny Town – A place where people care'. This would set out a theme that could then be looked at to see what could be changed to make the town a better place. Using the theme, the changes should be fairly obvious, although of course the Mayor knows and reminds everyone else that it will take time to identify them, and it is vital to hear what everyone has to say. Mind you, with a clear and agreed theme, agreeing changes would be quicker than without one. If clear examples of what is not right today can be given, even the conservative townsfolk would eventually agree that changes are required.

Perhaps there are several elderly people in the town that are lonely but not being cared about, or there is an uncared for park. The Mayor would work with the townspeople agreeing short, medium and long-term actions and goals for the town. Because the townsfolk believe and want their town to be a caring one they would agree that changes need to be made and, because they negotiated what changes are needed by consensus, they have ownership of them. They want to make the changes so they get on with them.

This is an example of management by democracy and implementation by autocracy. The townsfolk have chosen their course of action and therefore they want to carry out the changes. Okay, achieving consensus required a lot of patience but even a bad idea implemented well (because everybody wanted to do it) is far more effective than a good idea implemented badly (because people felt forced to do it).

The townsfolk (your staff) also relate to the town (your business) because it has values that they have set out and want. They know its special and want to be a part of it. Other people with these values will want to settle in the town, further increasing the community's strength around these values, and it is obvious as Mayor which ones not to take, as their values are not aligned (easier recruitment). New developments in the town are chosen sensitively to the values avoiding poorly directed effort and focus (avoids poor diversification/creates focus).

Even when the town is a good one and the townsfolk are rightly proud, the one thing the Mayor must do is to ensure that the town is constantly seeking to improve and change. Perhaps reflecting other developments, in other towns that are suitable, or new townspeople's needs. To achieve this, the Mayor would need to remind people that they are rightly proud of what they have achieved, that they did not achieve that without changing and by being complacent.

When people have the same values, share the same overall goal and respect each other and the boss, you have the makings of a strong well co-ordinated team. People don't work in isolation but are dependent on each other. Like a chain is as strong as its weakest point. When you start a business make a detailed plan of the sort of people you are going to need around you. Pick people that have a passion for the business and build a 'club' that they can all be a member of and feel committed to. Make sure that the values in the early stage are right for the business. For example, if your business needs ambitious, flexible people who always put the customer first, recruit people who share these values as well to do the job.

A cultural set of values is a formula for training, recruiting, creating a momentum, which comes back to a simple system. A set of values that support the corporate vision and objectives. This was a key finding in the pioneering book, *'In Search of Excellence'* which studied major successful companies to see what they did that was different and worked. A business with a core set of values that all share will create more passion, excitement, respect, loyalty, esprit de corps and, of course, it will become more successful. Look at successful businesses around you and you find that they have a clear set of values. They have a success formula. Customers and buyers see it and value it.

Leader/managers in the real world

Theoretical rules are fine, however the reality is that running a business is intensely time-consuming. Where do you get the time to do all that? It is not unusual particularly for owner/managers to find they are in control of strategy, management, marketing, production, finances and sales. Unfortunately these are probably too many responsibilities and they will get in the way of expanding the business. The key is to start building a team as soon as you can and delegating, ensuring that you build in strong controls. In our opinion the leader/manager (unless they resign) should never delegate strategy and should always keep a hand in marketing and people management. Strong financial control can be delegated entirely but check and double check the reports you are given and insist on controls.

Many entrepreneurs find there is no choice but to start as a one-man band and they then rapidly become used to doing everything. In reality the ones that move on quickly from that stage bring in experts in areas as soon as they have the resources to afford to do so. An entrepreneur is thus the catalyst that brings resources together, rather than an expert in any one of them.

Warning signs of when leadership is lacking

The signs can all be summarized under the heading 'motivation level'. At the top-level phones ring and are answered nearly immediately, people move with urgency and energy, with a smile on their face. There is both financial and personal success. If you want to know whether there is good leadership just ask the team.

Symptom	Cause	Possible quick-fixes
Over-content team	Good is never good enough! What's next? They need to know they are excelling but there is more required. The best teams drive the leadership, not the other way round.	Ask the team what it should do next for more success.
Small 'things to do' list	Suggests lack of pro-activity and purely reactive team/manager/leader	Brainstorm
Productive team only when boss present	Team lack motivation themselves, it only comes from being driven by management. Management probably operates by fear motivation. Also unable to work on the business as always has to be present for performance.	Implement systems and procedures. Brainstorm and create pro-active new ideas, not historically undertaken 'things to do' lists. Delegate accountability
High staff turnover	If people leave regularly and willingly they are not happy at work. This means they probably obtain low self-esteem and self-actualization in work. Whilst financial is also a factor the majority of people would actually put these drivers over money. Entrepreneurs sometimes miss this because they are often very money-driven themselves and can't understand people who are not motivated by cash alone.	Ask yourself and your team why they are not motivated and start making changes. Give them responsibility, invest in training, take time to understand and respect their goals.
Lack of ideas	Culture is not innovative. Management suppresses (bad), steals (ultimate sin) or fails to ask for ideas (poor).	Admit it to the staff, apologize and ask for ideas and help to solve the problem
Management always fire-fighting	Leader/managers should be working on the business (and very busy at that). Not very busy doing day-to-day tasks and worst fire-fighting. Caused by poor planning, organization, delegation and anticipation.	Go the extra mile for a concentrated duration to work on the systems and organization to create order. It may mean working very hard as you are both working on putting out fires as well as a system to avoid them but issues will ease off.
Poor long term profits	Business environments change and investments are required. So there are times when profits are either limited or occasionally a loss after an investment. This is fine short term so long as it is tightly controlled. Poor long-term profits are caused by a poor plan, lack of vision, poor productivity and uncontrolled cost.	Stop. If it is not working then don't keep on doing the same thing. Is the plan right? How can you increase profits without increasing costs? What significant changes can you make?

Leadership on purchase

A significant number of acquisitions fail to meet the expectations of the buyer. This is predominantly because the buyers overestimate their ability to change the business. This ultimately means they failed to get the people they are buying to change. Buyers carry out a significant amount of financial and legal due diligence but rarely do they carry out a cultural assessment. Essential questions for the buying management prior to purchasing a company should include:

- How flexible is this team we are buying, and are they used to and excited by change?
- What changes do we want to make?
- How receptive will they REALLY be to these changes?
- Do this team share the same values as me/us/our buying organization?
- What do this team believe in and want out of life?
- How will this team relate to new managements?
- What are the exiting parties' management styles compared to ours?
- Will the team we are buying listen to us, and how should we best communicate to them during this uncertain time (a sale)?
- Can I/we/my organization work with these people?
- Are there any differences in terms (salary/holidays) between my team and this team we are buying?
- If they are key, how can I lock them in (get the vendor to pay them a bonus or performance payment/share options)?

Leadership succession

Leaders/managers need to be dedicated to build a successful business. This by its nature means their contribution is crucial and central. The danger is that the business always then relies on this central role. This undermines long-term success and is almost impossible to manage when selling a business. A good business must be able to stand-alone without you. The leader/manager's job is to create superstars, not to be a superstar. Ultimately when you build a strong business your job is to put yourself out of a job.

Imagine the domineering parent, nurturing, disciplining, teaching, guiding, challenging, encouraging their child for success and happiness and then never letting go. How successful would the child be once it reaches adulthood? It would feel suppressed, bullied and held back. The same principle applies for your business. In other words, once you have a blossoming mature teenage business, although your child will make mistakes it is time to let go. Accept that decisions will be made that are not yours but nevertheless are good ones and that the odd mistake will be made, but if you have put in good foundations the business will still flourish.

When it comes to a business sale, the key is to have good foundations that reduce key dependency on any one person. This means implementing systems, training, procedures, delegation, goals and grooming a team for succession with a clear sense of purpose. You are working on the business, not in it.

Summary

Leader/managers are not born. The approach can be adopted with a little thought, time, training and effort. Those that go this extra mile will create a business which drives them, rather than the other way round. This crucially makes the business both more successful and more valuable on sale.

"The speed of the leader is the speed of the gang."

Mary Kay Ash

chapter ten How to sell – Cashing in

TEN How to sell – Cashing in

"Change before you have to."

Jack Welch

Chapter focus

- Introduction
- Cashing your chips in
- How to sell
- Using an intermediary and advisor to sell your business
- Choosing an intermediary
- Rules for finding and managing buyers
- Structure of the deal
- The sale process (a summary)
- Where next?

Introduction

The time may come when it is right to sell and realize the value you have built up in your business. But how do you start, when is the best time to sell and what is involved? Selling your business is a nerve-racking high stakes game, especially for those who don't know what they are doing. Like any game the better you understand the rules and the stronger your strategy, the more likely you are to win. In this chapter our aim is to reduce nerves and help you understand how to get the best deal by handling the sale correctly at the best time.

Cashing your chips in

Picture the scene: you're at the casino and on the roll. The night is still young (ish) and the money is rolling in. Deep down you know the odds are stacked against you, but lady luck is with you. It's the bright lights and the fast life... let's just have one more bet, after all we are on a roll. Ah.... the luck is turning, the system is failing, the dice are falling against you. You have missed that chance; should have cashed in when things were on the up.

Okay, owning a business is a bit more calculated luck than a casino, but you get the point. Knowing when to duck out gracefully is very difficult. It is important not to get seduced by the fast life and your ego and be objective about the decision. Choose when to get out and don't let bad luck determine it.

There is an ideal time to sell a business. However, predicting this time is very difficult. We believe the best any mortal can hope for is a time when certain criteria are being met in the business to make a sale worthwhile. This to coincide with a seller's market when the economy is at a high and/or the industry you are in is at a high with strong perception and buyers looking for opportunities.

Firstly, let's examine the criteria. We have already covered a lot of this ground in Chapter 7 'Adding value', however it is an opportune moment to remind ourselves. The best time in our opinion is when the company offers buyers:

- Potential
- Economies of scale (cost savings)
- Synergies (such as cross-sales)
- A match with their strategy
- A niche business in a growing well-perceived business arena
- A buoyant market to grow in
- Clear, established profits obviously sustainable or growing
- Good systems and replaceable owner/management
- Clean due diligence (no legal issues/tidy paperwork) and matters in good order

Often this time is the time when the seller is finally reaping the rewards of their efforts and they can still see continued growth. They are therefore perhaps understandably reticent to let go of the venture, but hanging on too long can be dangerous. If the company keeps growing will you be under-capitalized again, will you need second tier management? Will the competition get smarter? Will this start increasing pressure on the business (and you) and reduce profits in future years? It is possible all of these things might occur under the owner/manager, but may not occur if the business is sold to corporate owners. They are a risk to the owner/manager if they decide to hang on for continued growth, but they are unlikely to worry corporate purchasers.

When deciding whether to sell, greed should be avoided, and in our experience realism, pragmatism and clear non-emotive thinking is required to make the decision whether the time is right to sell. That is not to say of course that we don't want a fair price!

The time should also coincide with when it is personally right for you. Does it matter if the buyer goes on to bigger and better things with your business? If the purchaser goes on to make your business a 'star' you might think 'I could have done that', but was the sum being offered right at the time and did it seem right both from a business and personal perspective at that time? If so, it was right. What happens after is not in your control and other factors will affect it. Knowing when to stay and when to let go is all about stepping back and seeing clearly both from a personal and business strategic viewpoint. You may get it right, you may not, but if you have done your best thinking then you did what seemed right at the time. If a sale enables you to get on with what you want it is right.

Predicting a buoyant market is also important. The market for private companies does not seem to fluctuate as much as the corporate environment, but there are peaks and troughs like any stock or property market. Interestingly, the larger the business the higher the fluctuations, perhaps relating more closely to stock markets also comprising of larger enterprises. To predict markets the best we can all do is seek clarity. Look at the trends. Ask for professionals' opinions. Read international and trade press. Are interest rates up? What is the legislative environment for your business? Are new technologies coming in? What are the demographics of your customers? Is the world economy growing or stagnant?

"In any moment of decision the best thing you can do is the right thing. The worst thing you can do is nothing."

Theodore Roosevelt

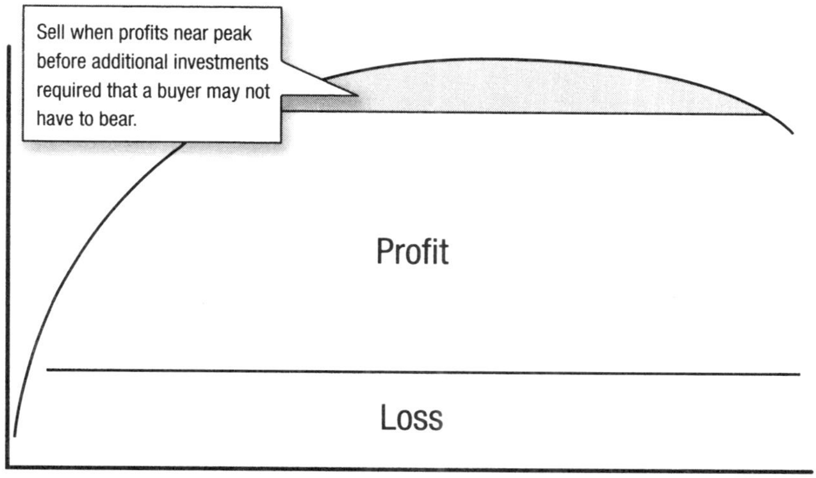

You never know, get the timing right and you might just have enough to spend a few nights in a casino.

How to sell

Now you have decided the right time to sell is upon you, have a number of options available to find a buyer and handle a sale. These are:

- To seek a trade buyer directly through your own efforts
- To wait until a trade buyer approaches you and makes a direct offer
- Approaching people you know
- To employ an intermediary to seek a buyer and handle the transaction for you
- To set up a management buy-out with your existing team
- To seek a management buy-in
- To float on the stock exchange (IPO)

Selling direct

By the time most owner/managers have a venture that is profitable and saleable, most will have learnt a lot about the business world and are possibly capable of handling a sale without help. However, despite on the surface being cheaper, there are some intrinsic problems. Firstly, the time involved to do the job well is significant and this can result in the direct seller taking their eye off the ball and damaging their businesses goodwill (and price) in the process. Secondly, there is no substitute for the experience, contacts, knowledge of the market and expertise a capable advisor will bring. Cheap can in the long-term prove very expensive and, after all, would a surgeon operate on himself?

We know there is an argument that, as intermediaries, we are biased, but it is not as if we are frightened of giving away our expertise. Would we have written this book if we were? We completely and passionately believe that without help (from a good advisor) the time wasted, the lack of resources and the inability to be objective is highly, highly damaging. The benefits of using a good intermediary far outweigh the costs involved. We examine advisors in depth in the next section.

Being approached directly by buyers can be attractive, however it is reactive not pro-active so the timing is hit and miss. In addition, a direct approach can bring canny corporate buyers who have read the rulebook as well and who will therefore try and gain advantage over a seller. They will be hoping to catch naïve sellers without advisors and apply pressure to get them to accept early and potentially low first offers. The biggest issue with the direct approach is that it does not allow the market to best decide the price through a competitive environment. Again, see 'Choosing an intermediary and advisor' below for more details.

Approaching people you know

It may be possible to sell the business to a known contact or friend, however this has many of the same problems as selling to a direct approach to you. Actually, it is worse because it can be harder to establish the contact's financial position. Imagine asking John or Jane at the Golf Club if he or she has the money. Can they afford it, and are they really serious?

Many friends will have looked at your venture, and have always fancied the idea. After all, you have done well from it. Often friends' initial reaction when approached is positive but once they start seriously thinking about it and understand what is really involved, our experience is, more often than not, they get cold feet. This is especially the case if they are not already entrepreneurs. Also, will they blame you if a purchase proves a bad investment after sale? Perhaps they are not as good as you, or the market changes right at the time you get out.

Contacts can be better – particularly suppliers or competitors; however, maintaining confidentiality is a serious issue here.

Management buy-out/buy-in

A management buy-out (MBO) or management buy-in (MBI) is a viable option, particularly for companies with a strong balance sheet to enable highly leveraged finance. A management buy-out is where the existing management team raises finance, buys and then runs the business in which they were previously employed. A buy-in is where a manager or management team, from outside the company, raises the necessary finance to buy the company, and takes it over.

Buy-ins present the problem of where do you find the manager to buy-in? You are back to finding a party directly through marketing, or better, relying on an intermediary with experience and knowledge of the market. Buy-outs are more interesting. You know the party or parties (your team). Should you approach them and see what they can do before exploring a trade deal?

It is a very awkward situation. Telling the team you are thinking of selling can be very damaging to morale and the goodwill of the business. The uncertainty can be highly damaging. Certainly if you do choose to talk to your existing management be very selective and bind them confidentially (see confidentiality below). Preferably, sound them out informally over time without being too specific. Appraisals can be an ideal time to ask the odd discrete question/hint and see what response you get. Only approach those who you know could access funds of say 10% of the value of the business. Lower than this and they are unlikely to have a hope of raising the funds.

The opposite argument is that if you don't offer it to management and just explore the trade sale, you have ignored a potential buyer and may, if you achieve a trade sale, have damaged your goodwill leaving a buyer with obviously disgruntled managers. Our experience is that an intermediary should be employed to explore both options, however, on balance we generally prefer trade buyers as they are usually in a position to pay more.

The major challenge for management buy-outs is likely to be raising finance. Individuals, particularly historically salaried employees (you know how much you pay them), are unlikely to be high net worth, and therefore they will probably have much less to put in than a trade buyer. Trade buyers usually have surplus profits sitting in reserve for an acquisition, and therefore they may and should be able and perhaps willing to pay more. They are also usually able to obtain economies of scale making the venture potentially worth more than if it is left as a stand alone business. Trade buyers will usually make more money out of your business than you can.

Banks are supportive to management buy-outs, particularly where the team has a track record of being left to run the company and deliver growth historically. Also where the company offers security for any funding. That is, the purchase includes a strong balance sheet and offers good security if things go wrong. Banks don't really like financing goodwill. It's intangible and has a habit of disappearing when things go wrong.

Advice should be sought early on by the management team regarding their financing prospects. Sellers should be aware that it could become quite legally complex, particularly if the assets of the company are to be used as security to raise funds. Management buy-outs are also risky for the buyer. Because the purchase is so highly financed the company is likely to be highly sensitive to interest rate hikes, and struggling to make repayments is common.

The biggest issue with MBOs is that if the existing management team are unsuccessful in their bid, one of the business's greatest assets can become its greatest liability. They should be approached with caution and we believe firmly that trade sales should be explored via a professional intermediary.

Management buy-ins (MBIs) are very similar to seeking a trade sale, because you have to find the manager, although they are highly leveraged deals to outside buyers typically managers, in the trade. Also BIMBOs or Brought in Management Buy Outs can be considered. These are where a finance house has identified an acquisition and brings in a manager to run the business for them after purchase. Both MBIs and BIMBOs rely on direct approaches, unless an intermediary is employed to seek such a party.

Using an intermediary and advisor to sell your business

In building your business, you have undoubtedly made invaluable contacts within the industry. Most probably you have also had numerous occasions to develop your negotiating skills, perhaps even acquiring a company yourself. You would therefore not be surprised to learn that many business owners decide to sell their businesses by themselves. Selling a business can however be a very complex and time-consuming proposition. There are many legal, tax, accounting and regulatory issues to address. In addition, there is the matter of finding the appropriate buyer for your business and then negotiating and structuring the most advantageous deal.

The sale of your business is likely to be one of the most important economic decisions you make, and you usually only have one chance to get it right. A sale (or merger/MBO) is therefore best handled with experienced professional help. Experience, expertise and resources are essential.

An intermediary will act on behalf of a seller and frequently both seller and purchaser will engage their own advisors. Their basic role is to search for an appropriate purchaser for a business and then negotiate and structure a deal for the sale of the business. An intermediary will work with a client throughout the sale process, from preparing the initial valuation through to the close of the sale. The main benefits of using an intermediary are listed below.

Experience and expertise

It has probably taken you years to develop the skills necessary to build a successful business. Likewise a good advisor will have spent a great deal of time developing the expertise, processes, technical skills, knowledge of the market and, in particular, data resources to efficiently find purchasers and manage a sale or merger.

The maximum deal value

Purchasers will place different values upon a business according to their sector, infrastructure and strategy. The best buyer who will place the highest value on your business will have a 'we want, we need' motivation driven by many strategic aspects. A good advisor will recognize this and seek the best strategic buyers to optimize your transaction.

Research, knowledge of buyers and creating competitive environments

The best buyer for your business is a strategic buyer who achieves economies of scale and synergy. One who understands the expansion prospects in your business and has a vision for both their and your company combined. A good advisor will identify a number of strategic buyers by recognizing and matching their criteria to yours. They will usually seek 'offers' rather than name a price, enabling the market to best decide the value. Good advisors will also seek to create a competitive environment with more than one buyer to drive your price forward. This is similar to an auction approach and requires very careful managing. Buyers are more likely to believe you have interested parties if you use a good capable advisor.

Valuation

Advisors' knowledge of comparative transactions through real experience will help in understanding whether offers are reasonable or not. Remember, valuations are subjective and depend on who the buyer is.

Grooming

We all like to think our business is tidy and in order. However, little changes can make a big difference when selling. An advisor will educate you on buyer needs and what makes a difference, enabling you to groom your business pre-sale to maximize the value.

Confidentiality

For commercial businesses (non-retail) it is vital for a sale to be handled confidentially to avoid loss of goodwill and disruption to the business. This means buyers should be vetted and confidentiality undertakings obtained prior to disclosing who the business is for sale, or any key information. A good sale adviser will manage this process for you working closely with you, advising you of details of interested parties. Not only will this protect your goodwill, it should avoid you wasting time with tyre kicker buyers (dreamers).

Negotiation skills

A clear head and strong nerve are essential when securing the best deal, but it is hard to maintain this if you are acting by yourself, especially when the stakes are high. An advisor will create a buffer to create flexibility, reduce disagreement and manage negotiations to your best advantage. Years of experience should help them spot buyer tactics and combat them effectively. It will also enable them to ensure the right deal is structured; one that is more likely to complete.

Management time savings

From research and vetting buyers to managing confidentiality, information releases and negotiations, selling a business is very time-consuming. Employing the right advisor should reduce your time involvement and the pressures on you, enabling you to concentrate on your business and continue to ensure its goodwill.

Choosing an intermediary (broker/advisor)

Now that you understand the benefits, how do you choose an intermediary? To look for an intermediary ask business friends for recommendations, or look in your National Financial Press, depending on which country you are in. Many brokers will also contact you over time. Keep their contact details in anticipation of when you are ready to sell. Preferably touch base with them well in advance of being ready and discuss with them your plan. The good ones will have ideas and resources that may help you. It is a good idea to talk to two or three potential brokers to get a judgement for the differences in approach and which advisor most suits you.

There are lots of different types of advisors and not all sale advisers can help with a sale for you. Many will have a focus on different size or type of business to yours. Advisers also offer different service levels and abilities. As a general rule you get what you pay for, although we will look at how intermediaries charge later.

It is preferable that the advisor has experience of your trade, although not essential. If you have a niche business a strong commercial acumen will suffice. As for size of business, you should be able to tell from the intermediary's existing portfolio the types of businesses they usually handle.

Accountants can and do sell businesses, however many don't have a specialist division with the resources and experience to help. Far better a firm who specializes purely in transactions or at least has a dedicated division with significant resources allocated to this task. Also, be wary of firms with a financing and tax focus. Whilst these are good skills to have, without a purchaser (or several) there are no funds for them to raise or tax to save.

Look for:

- Specialists in transactional work
- A proven advisor with a track record
- An understanding of your business
- National (and if you are big enough, international) resources
- Expertise and experience
- A focus on maximizing deal value
- A complete, personal start to finish service (not just introducer/finders* but advisors who will structure and manage the deal for you)
- Strong research and marketing focus to find the right buyers
- Practical, objective and realistic advice
- A straightforward, keep it simple approach
- People you can relate to and who will listen to your needs
- A cost-effective (not cheap) results-driven service
- Fees mainly on success

The larger the business the more international resources may become relevant, even if this is just access to international data resources.

As well as the firm you choose being able, it is also important to get on with the people in the business. Will the person whom you meet be the one that handles the sale? If not, can you meet them? If so, what are their team and resources like? Find an excuse to visit their offices and get a feel for the organization. Your business is potentially your largest asset and a sale must be handled right from the start. It is worth taking the time to choose the right professionals to help you.

---

* Finder organizations will usually have an advertising-led focus and just introduce buyers leaving you to the negotiations. Finding the buyer is only half the job. Getting the right buyer and deal structure and making sure it completes is vital. If you insist on using a finder make sure you pay half the price.

Fees will vary depending on the advisor (and percent depending on the currency) but, as we have said, as a rule of thumb you get what you pay for. A good advisor will have a flexible approach to fees to meet your needs, however they will also want to ensure that there is strong incentive for them to deliver the result you want, and of course like all businesses, profitably. This can mean that cheaper firms will not be dedicating the resources or service levels to really make a difference and deliver the maximum sale for you. Most firms will charge the majority of their fees on a success commission basis, usually a percentage of the sale price achieved, payable on completion; a few will work on a time billed basis only.

Nearly all the quality firms will charge some form of initial fee at the time of your instruction to sell. This fee should be reasonable, maintaining the majority of the sale fee on success, to ensure their motivation is driven by your needs. This initial fee will provide them the confidence of your serious intent to sell, enabling the advisor to spend the significant amount of time and provide the dedicated resources that selling for maximum value requires. Selling is neither a short or easy job and requires professional, expert, intelligent and capable people to be done right.

The success fee can be structured in a number of ways. It can be a flat percentage of the sale price, or a scaled percentage rising or declining. Sellers keen to provide incentives to the broker to exceed initial forecast valuations and secure top dollar usually negotiate a rising scale, although this will need to be balanced by the advisor's base costs which they will need to cover to ensure getting involved in the transaction is profitable for them.

The sale of a business can be a very time-consuming process. An intermediary's role is to relieve you of most of the burdens and pressures associated with the sale of your business. Nonetheless you will also have a key role in how you help represent the business to a purchaser, particularly in respect of the quality of sale information the intermediary is able to provide.

You will need to stay active and informed of the sale progress throughout because, in the end, you will make all of the decisions. Although each sale is different, an intermediary will generally handle the following functions:

- Grooming advice (often charged separately to sale service)
- Determine a target sale price and valuation of your business using comparative and financial techniques in order to help you with your financial planning

- Prepare a sales information memorandum, detailing your business's operations and activities. For commercial ventures this should exclude company specific information to maintain confidentiality.
- Identify through research and marketing potential acquirers
- Vet and approach prospective purchasers
- Inform you at every step of activity and companies that are interested, particularly at information release stages
- Manage information releases to purchasers, including managing confidentiality documentation
- Sell the benefits of an acquisition
- Secure more than one interested party
- Attend and chair viewing and negotiation meetings
- Create a competitive environment with more than one buyer to maximize price
- Negotiate the transaction to the best price/deal structure
- Aim to exceed target price and minimize your tax bill/costs
- Preparing 'heads of terms' (summary of key points to deal prior to definitive legal agreement)
- Working with solicitors and all other parties to ensure the sale process follows through to completion.

Pick an intermediary for their knowledge of the market, research skills, database, buyers, marketing and negotiating skills in completing a deal. If they are good (if you have any doubts obtain references and insist on seeing their offices) then the fee they charge you will be offset by the higher price and the deal terms they obtain.

Example sale or merger process									
G Month	**1**	**2**	**3**	**4**	**5**	**6**	**7**	**8**	**9**
Research	■	■	■	■	■	■	■	■	
Approach confidentially			■	■	■				
Initial meetings			■	■	■				
Invite offers				■	■	■			
Negotiate offers				■	■	■	■		
Create competitive environment				■	■	■	■		
Agree best deal with best party						■	■		
Manage through to completion							■	■	■
Note: This is a typical timeline. The process can be speeded up. However, this can have an adverse affect on the number of buyers that can be found. The above assumes no regulatory permission or grooming is required for the transaction.									

Rules for finding and managing buyers

If you are using, as recommended, an intermediary they will carry out this job; however, if you are looking for a buyer directly you should both research and market for a buyer. Advertise in trade, entrepreneur and national press. As well as advertising think about and then research the type of person or corporation that would have an interest and benefit in owning your business. Create a shortlist including the name of the person responsible for acquisitions if it is a corporate. Then confidentially approach the shortlist in writing and follow it up. To create your shortlist, network amongst your current contacts, consider suppliers, customers, use the Internet, trade fairs, trade lists and company database resources. Individual or institutional investors may also be considered. Your approach should not mention your location or company name to maintain confidentiality, and you may prefer to use a filter address.

Not wishing to demean it but selling, like any negotiation, is a bit of a game. Okay, in this case a very important and high stakes and stress game. This means it is vital to have a good game strategy and a coach (intermediary). As with any game there are rules you need to understand and play by. We have set out a few below:

Rule 1: Create a competitive environment

- Research, shortlist and confidentially approach likely buyers
- Find more than one willing and able buyer, preferably strategic
- Look for buyers who cannot refuse the offer (this usually means seeking market sector dominance or entry)
- Look for buyers with 'we need/we want' motivation
- Create a semi-auction process between the buyers, but don't be too blatant. Buyers generally hate hardball.

Rule 2: Let the market decide

(Only suitable for larger non-property orientated commercial ventures)

- Seek offers rather than quote a price. The buyer may place a higher value on the business than you
- Politely decline requests for a price (for smaller companies you may eventually have to give some indication)
- Point out that the value is different to every buyer.

Rule 3: Play your cards close to your chest

- Retain key confidential information to the last
- Secure a confidentiality undertaking
- Never refuse to give information, just say not yet
- Vet buyers and avoid tyre kickers (timewasters) or Unicorn hunters (in search of the mythical).

Rule 4: Never underestimate the other players

- Remember, buyers have read the rule book (and are often experienced players)
- Win on the big points, lose on the small ones
- Watch your opponents like a hawk
- Spot buyer moves and tactics.

Rule 5: Understand what you are selling

- Know your strengths and weaknesses
- Put yourself in your buyers' shoes and think like them
- Present the quality of your business and it's systems
- Communicate the investments you have made (not your time)
- Be clear on what makes your business valuable
- Promote your niche or unique selling point
- Promote your business, not yourself (it needs to work without you).

Rule 6: Start how you intend to finish

- Be prepared with all likely information required to hand*
- Keep it simple, direct, honest and factual
- Be approachable and helpful
- Understand buyers' needs and listen to their views
- Work with the buyer to achieve a sale, not against them (collaborative)
- Aim at a win/win (where both parties are happy). You are more likely to achieve a win yourself
- Be objective (buyers prefer facts rather than beliefs).

There are lots of other rules, indeed we could write a book on negotiation rules alone, however we have, we hope, chosen the most important. Unfortunately selling is one game where practice is not easy to come by. In our experience the usual winners are the ones who have undertaken the most preparation, which they combine with an adaptability and speed. In the military context it is also important to remember that no plan survives first engagement with the enemy. You need to adapt it as the game moves along to gain best advantage.

There is a common tendency in buyers to comment that they are not paying for potential because 'you can't value it'. This is not always correct. The nature of purchasing goodwill is in purchasing tomorrow's income, therefore it is an immediate potential. Indeed, a business that is expandable at a rate of 40% per year is worth considerably more than a business

* refer to the due diligence checklist in Chapter 5.

that is expandable at a rate of 10-15% per year, even if the profits and assets are the same today. Prepare a case for why your business is valuable.

Remember, buyers will have read the rulebook and often have played the game before. It is therefore important that even with honourable buyers (most are), they will still be trying to gain the best position for themselves. It is human nature to try and win, and they will try and gain points. If you give points away you will make it easy for them. There are some very easy mistakes that can be made:

- Showing desperation (even if you are)
- Talking to much (showing your hand too much)
- Staying when you should walk away
- Threatening to walk away, but not actually doing it (obvious bluff)
- Negotiating directly rather than via your intermediary (if employed). Remember, buyers will try and undermine your intermediary; it's to their best advantage.
- Forgetting to think like the buyer. What is their plan and how is it best to handle it?
- Getting too friendly. The good buyers often use charm as a tactic.
- Allowing fear, ego, pride or greed to get in the way of realism. Emotions are a human blessing but when it comes to the negotiation table they create havoc.

Whilst you are seeing prospective buyers you also still have to run the business. Staff can wonder what is going on and how they are likely to be affected. Uncertainty tends to produce a negative motivation, even if the most likely outcome is an improvement in their conditions. Near a sale, a keen buyer will obviously want to meet key staff. Before you do this we recommend that you hold meetings away from your premises. Use your home, consultant's offices, hotel lobby or meet over lunch in a restaurant or public house. Staff need to be talked to at an appropriate time and, in the small to mid market, we believe this is the last minute. Be aware however, that there may in some countries be a legal obligation to consult with staff earlier on. Please check with your lawyer.

Structure of the deal

One crucial element of a sale and therefore consequently vital detail to tie down at the negotiation stage is the structure of the deal. The heads of terms should cover the sale structure comprehensively. Companies and businesses are complex with many legal aspects and entities. Will the sale be a share transfer or what is known as an asset sale? Companies have a choice, but sole traders and Partnerships can only do asset sales. They have no shares and effectively the goodwill and assets belong personally to the owners.

Asset sales (Partnerships/sole traders)

It is important to define what is included. Typically the fixed assets are included plus a sum for goodwill. The vendor will retain their cash, debtors and creditors up to the date of completion. The buyer will help collect any debtor payments and pass these on to the seller. The seller will settle off any debt and keep the bank account. Usually the net of these is a positive figure and therefore can form an addition to the price. The seller will need to account for working capital as a consequence on top of the sale price.

It is important to also define the fixed assets. Are the Partners' cars included? Usually not. A detailed inventory of equipment and fixed assets will need to be provided. It will be expected that the sale will be with assets unencumbered of any charges.

Some third party supplier, contract arrangements or leases may be awkward to take over and transfer on an 'asset sale'. Often these arrangements are in the personal name of the owner and they will need to be assigned to the new owner. This will require the approval of the third party who may be awkward. This should be looked into pre-sale. Property leases in particular require the new owner to have a good covenant before they can be assigned over to him or her.

Asset sales (from companies)

These are the same legal and financial structure as the above, however the one fundamental difference is that the company has elected to sell its assets, not the sole traders or Partners. This means the company is the vendor, and the proceeds will go into the company. To transfer the name the selling company will change its name on completion, and the buyer will adopt this name immediately. As far as customers are concerned it is seamless, but the same third party arrangements as above may be awkward to take over, transfer.

In the UK (where we are based) companies opting to sell their assets are not (at the time of writing) usually tax effective and it is best avoided by the shareholder sellers, as a double tax charge is usually incurred. Consequently it usually only happens if they have no choice and the buyer dictates it. Buyers will dictate for two reasons:

1 It is tax effective for buyers to acquire assets and goodwill rather than shares, as they can depreciate/amortize the assets.

2 It reduces their liabilities. When buyers acquire shares they buy the company as an entity, lock stock and barrel. This means they buy all its current known, and many historic and unknown, liabilities (skeletons), although usually they will demand warranties as a contingency from the seller against 'skeletons in the cupboard'. They don't always know what those warranties should cover. In addition a retrospective claim is hassle and often fails to compensate adequately for the true cost and time wasted as a result of the problem.

Ultimately, when considering assets versus shares, the seller normally wins. How can a buyer ask him or her to incur a double tax charge? Sometimes smart buyers will still insist on assets but pay more to help the seller with their tax bill.

Share transfers

As we examined above, the liabilities known or otherwise get transferred with the shares, therefore the most complicated aspect of these is agreeing a legal contract with sufficient warranties and indemnities to protect the buyer against such unknowns. There can however, be other complications, in particular for smaller companies. Many smaller companies, although in theory separate entities from the shareholders, are interlinked. Often personal property outside the company is used to secure lending where the company is unable to stand on its own feet. Or landlords will insist on directors' guarantees on leases, or there are directors' loans supporting the company. Buyers will have to sort these aspects out, and consequently, particularly if they have to put forward extra money or security, they can have an impact on the price.

Possible deal structures

Business sales, mergers and acquisitions are rarely structured all in cash. For a number of reasons including tax, financing, buyer hedging and maximization of value, deals can be structured. We have set out a guide below for some of the more common structures:

- Cash
- Deferred payments
- Retentions
- Performance related payments (PRP)
- Earn outs
- Elevator deals
- Shares
- Mergers

1. Cash in full on completion

'All Cash' on completion deals can and often are achieved. Buyers are happy as they have immediate ownership, and sellers are happy as they have a minimum risk on the payment. 'All Cash' is ideal as a seller if you are retiring, the business is not dependent on you, and you categorically want an immediate exit. However, it may not be the best way to maximize the value. If the business is dependent on the vendor or has other high risks associated, one key contract or supplier for example, it may not even be achievable as buyers seek to hedge their handover risk.

2. Deferred payment

Deferred payments are where a percentage of the price is paid to the vendor on a fixed basis over a fixed period of time, usually with interest. The deferred part of the deal is effectively a vendor loan and is usually put in place to help the buyer finance the purchase, particularly if banks are unsupportive. It may also enable some of the price to be paid out of future profits. The purchase price is defined from the outset, a proportion of the price is payable on completion and the remainder is payable over a period of time. In a 'heads of terms' (the document that sets out an agreed deal) it might appear as follows:

Item	**Amount**	**Payable**	Note
Initial payment	£1,000,000	On completion	For the purchase of 100% of the share capital of the business.
Deferred payments	£500,000	Payable over 2 years following completion	8 equal quarterly payments of £62,500 will be made. The first payment of £62,500 will be made 3 months after completion, and a further quarterly payment of £62,500 will be made every quarter up to and including 24 months after completion.
Total	£1,500,000		

When should a seller accept a deferred payment structure?

Only if:

- They are happy with the value of the initial payment if in a 'worst case scenario' that was all they were to receive
- Personal guarantees are given on the deferred amount, preferably bank guarantees. If they are available could you get the cash instead?)
- Some form of security in the form of a debenture or additional security from the buyer's freehold

3. Retention

Retentions are also a form of deferred payment. The idea is that the purchaser pays all the money on completion but retains a proportion in an escrow account held by the vendor's solicitors, in lieu of certain events. It may be just whilst the final net asset value of a company is calculated at completion, or in lieu of a contract being renewed. Retentions work well because sellers can see their money, but buyers do have a means of straightforward claw-back in certain pre-defined eventualities if they need it.

4. Performance related payments (PRP)

An initial payment is made on completion and then secondary performance related payments made subject to certain performance caveats. These are often used to help:

- The buyer 'hedge' risks and finance the deal from future profits
- The seller 'maximize' the deal by linking it to future expected growth.

Example 1 PRP: In the first example we have assumed that the business being purchased has historically had a turnover of circa £2,000,000 per annum, and that the PRP is going to be linked to the business continuing at this level.

Item	Amount	Payable	Note
Initial payment	£1,000,000	On completion	For the purchase of 100% of the share capital of the business.
PRP	£500,000 (estimated)	Payable over 2 years following completion	8 equal quarterly payments will be made commencing 3 months after completion, and continuing every quarter up to and including 24 months after completion. Each quarterly payment will be calculated as 12.5% of the turnover achieved in the quarter immediately preceding each payment.
Target	£1,500,000		

The rationale behind this is that the business turns over £2 million per annum, therefore should turn over £4 million in the two years following completion. The target PRP is £500,000, which is 12.5% of the expected turnover over the two-year period. If the business under-performs the seller will receive less than the target price, but if the business exceeds its targets the seller will receive more that the target price. Sometimes upper and/or lower limits are imposed on such deals, and sometimes there is a minimum level at which the business must perform, and if it fails to do so no PRP is made.

Example 2 PRP: In the second example below, the business has a contract with a client that contributes a significant amount to the business's turnover. We have assumed that the contract is renewed annually:

Item	Amount	Payable	Note
Initial payment	£1,000,000	On completion	For the purchase of 100% of the share capital of the business.
PRP	£500,000 (conditional)	Estimated 6 months after completion	The business currently has a one year contract to supply goods to 'ABC Group Ltd.' which is due to expire approximately 6 months after completion. If the business is successful in winning a renewal of this contract a PRP of £500,000 will be made on renewal of the contract.
Target	£1,500,000		

When should a seller accept a performance related payment?

ONLY IF:

- The operation can be clearly ring-fenced as a stand alone venture, enabling the policing of performance so the value of the payment due can be checked
- Access of the company's records can be given to the seller so they can 'police' the payments
- The buyer will issue statements regarding the payments
- Guarantees / security on the payment are available (as with deferred payments section 2 above)
- The performance caveat looks achievable based on forecasts. Is it based on current performance or growth?
- The PRP has been approached with caution. Who defines the profit and how? Once the business is out of the seller's hands, can they control costs?

5. Earn outs

These are effectively performance related payments where the seller is expected to stay and work to achieve the PRP through that work on a service contract. The idea is that the vendor has a financial incentive to help make a success of the business or the larger organization after sale.

6. Elevator deals (for ambitious sellers) – 'Cash some of your chips and keep playing'

Elevator deals provide a mechanism to link the purchase price of a business to its potential future value OR profits. An ongoing involvement in the business is required by the seller in order to drive and 'elevate' the value and profitability going forward. By retaining shares in their business or by taking shares from the buyer, sellers have the potential to truly maximize the overall value of the sale transaction.

Aren't elevator deals mergers?

No, because in the majority of deals a controlling interest changes hands. Many business owners would consider a merger but in reality a good one is hard to come by due to issues of control. One party will normally quite rightly want control, and the chances of exact equals meeting are hard. Let's face it, it's very difficult to run a business by committee, however democratic the organization is. Ultimately the buck has to stop somewhere and for truly effective visionary growth someone has to be leading, calling the shots.

Who do elevator deals work well for?

- Organizations with underdeveloped profits as a result of youth, lack of investment capital or where profits are being used for expansion. Consequently, if an outright sale is sought these companies will be under valued by the market.
- Businesses with a strong track record of growth and with good future potential.
- Young ambitious sellers with more to give who are willing to stay in the business and maximize their future potential.
- Companies where sustainability as an 'independent' is questionable due to lack of capital to invest or in a fast moving market.
- Sellers where the fun of the start-up has faded and they want a new challenge.

How does the buyer benefit?

- Getting in early (possibly cheaper) before the potential of the seller's company is realized.
- By helping increase the seller's chance of realizing potential.

- Through possible economies of scale between the combined companies, helping both businesses fulfil their future value and profitability after the deal.
- By having a controlling interest after an acquisition with the synergies of 1+1 = 3, that is the creation of a larger company with greater profits. Possibly even a size of company that may leapfrog the multiples; usually the bigger the profit the bigger the profit multiple used in valuation. Ultimately this leads to larger profits and greater shareholder value.
- By locking in the seller's employment, the chance of maintaining growth momentum is increased.
- By having the controlling interest. Mergers are really only a 'myth'; there is usually a lead party.

What are the typical characteristics of an elevator deal?

- A typical elevator deal will usually have at least some of the following characteristics:
- A price linked to the **future profits** of the business, not **past profits**, and possibly linked to the future capital value of the business in the form of a shareholding.
- A purchase in the region of 50% of the company enabling the vendor to 'bank a bit' now.
- The vendor is offered a percentage in the buyer's business or NEWCO formed. Usually there will be a plan again for a future exit to liquidate this minority shareholding, hopefully at a grown value, enabling the seller to 'elevate' a further capital sum.
- A good buyer/seller synergy makes the 'elevation' on offer of 1+1 = 3 appear achievable. The idea is that the two together will not only make more money, but potentially be worth more combined than the sum of the two individual parts.
- Ideally the deal will help the seller realize his potential by taking away the headache of running the business (Finance/HR) so they can grow it on their combined core strengths.
- The seller retains an active role in the business, probably as MD or Development Director enabling them to contribute to the growth and profitability of the business in the mid-term.

- A good solid service contract on commercial terms (usually salaried with car, pension, healthcare) being offered to the seller. A new employment agreement will be put in place with some entrenched rights so he cannot be easily dismissed.
- A typical elevation may be the proposed 'float' of the sellers' and buyers' combined business in the future.

When should a seller accept an elevator deal?

ONLY IF:

- They are happy that the 'upfront cash' payable on completion goes a good way to the current value of their business.
- They know that the shares or performance payments are 'ON RISK'. For instance there may be a 50/50 chance of achieving value. In Roulette red has a 48% chance of winning. Remember, a shareholding is only as valuable as the willingness of a third party to pay fair value for those shares.
- They like the buyer and want to get involved, truly believing the strategy is REALISTIC. The seller can relate to the buyer and the buyer's philosophy. Do the cultures fit? The question to ask is, "Can I work with this guy during the good and the bad times?" As part of this understanding the seller will need to understand that the target company is no longer solely his and he will need to work more collaboratively, being prepared to involve others. "How will I deal with a board meeting where my wishes may not carry the day?" On the other side of the coin, the buyer will also have to get used to the seller being involved in his business.
- The end game is thought through. How will you realize the future value of your holding? What are the realistic chances of a successful trade sale or floatation? Have you talked about the buyer's exit plans?
- They are prepared to work in the business for a few more years – "it's not retirement yet."
- They recognize their shareholding is today 'ON RISK' and they are willing to bank a bit now and take the remainder 'ON RISK' for the potential of maybe doubling their money again.
- They can explain their 'ON RISK' perception to their lawyers.

- The shares in the NEWCO or buyer's company are enhanced by a quality shareholder's agreement with caveats that:
  - Value the shares pro-rata
  - Offer first refusal to 'buy each other out' either on a voluntary transfer or a deemed transfer (for example on death and bankruptcy or ceasing to be an employee)
  - Cross-options if the seller dies ensuring the estate benefits from cash, not a minority shareholding. To ensure that the company or the other shareholder has the cash to acquire a deceased's shareholding it may be appropriate for a life policy to be put in place
  - A seat on the Board to reflect the shareholding
  - Agreed minority shareholding protection to ensure that the minority shareholder has rights of veto over certain fundamental matters.
- The minimum net asset value caveats are agreed in advance as protection if they are accepting shares in the buyer's company.

Elevator deal examples:

Example 1: A fast track company is valued on current profits today at £1.2 million. This is because the profits are being used to fund growth. An elevator deal is agreed with a buyer seeking an AIMS float in 2 years.		
£1,000,000	On completion	Cash and therefore secure.
£800,000	Preference shares	Preference shares with interest in 2 years. A preference share is secured by the company, but of course if all goes badly in the company they are worthless and impossible to redeem. Effectively this is a 2 years 'interest only' ON RISK loan to the buyer. This could be loan notes or a performance related payment on future profits.
£150,000	5% minority shareholding with good shareholder's agreement	5% at today's value is estimated to be £150,000 but of course shares can go up as well as down so this is ON RISK in order to hopefully be worth double the money or more (possibly even £500,000 after a float?).
£100,000	Salary plus pension, car and healthcare	

Example 2: A profitable technology business is currently valued at say £750,000 on profits, however it is heavily dependent on the vendor and therefore very hard to realize this value. In addition the market is moving quickly with the cost of 'development' becoming higher and as such hard for the business to stay independent and sustain revenue streams.		
£250,000	On completion	Cash and therefore secure.
Target £250,000+	20% minority shareholding with good shareholder's agreement	20% at today's value is estimated at £250,000 but of course shares can go up as well as down so this is ON RISK in order to hopefully be worth double the money or more (possibly even £500,000 after a float?).This is agreed subject to the buyers having a minimum net asset of £500,000.
£100,000	Salary + pension, car and healthcare	

'Elevator' summary

'Cash some of your chips and keep on playing' – Elevator deals provide sellers with the opportunity to bank half their money now 'in the casino', perhaps paying the mortgage off or buying basic financial independence (the ability to cease work on a modest lifestyle). With the other half they continue to 'gamble' with the aim of a big win and a potential to double this half again. Both parties need to enter into the arrangement with their eyes open, with similar objectives and end games. Through teamwork with the buyer, the seller may get the job back they enjoyed – developing the trade, rather than working on the business (accounts/HR and finances). The seller enjoys a new journey, having secured a future for the business and banking a base line. An interesting new concept...

7. Shares

We have already seen in elevator deals how some buyers and sellers will offer and accept shares (usually a minority shareholding) in some transactions despite the risks involved for either side. Some buyers may also just offer shares as a means to avoid using cash. These are in a way a form of deferred payments. In a private company in an illiquid market, sellers should approach these shareholdings with great caution. How do you value minority shareholdings and how do you sell them?

Shares in corporations floated on the stock market as Public Limited Companies (PLCs) are closer to cash and may have an interest to sellers. After all, subject to orderly market restrictions that will normally be placed on them, there is a liquid market which is public, thus enabling their sale. Some corporate buyers particularly of small PLCs will have to offer shares in order to help them raise funding from institutional investors. The idea is they can send the signal to the markets that the vendors are in on their plans, sharing the risks and prepared to help them; a key message for institutional investors to be prepared to offer funding. Don't forget, the true value of the shares is the quoted price less selling costs on the day they can be sold, not the day they are received at completion. Shares can go down as well as up.

8. Mergers

Parties may seek a merger. A merger is a combination of two or more businesses on an equal footing that results in the creation of a new reporting entity. The shareholders of the combining entities mutually share the risks and rewards of the new entity. In the SME market mergers are rare, as finding two companies with a shared vision and cultures that can be easily integrated often leads to the challenge of one party wanting a controlling share. This often stops these deals completing. Mergers are more likely to occur and are in fact more common in PLC's where shareholders are less attached both directly and emotionally to the running of the business. (NB: Avondale Group will not act in the sale and purchase of minority shareholdings.)

Tax and deal structures?

Depending in which tax environment (country/region) your business is sold, tax on any capital gain you make will probably be your biggest cost. The rule here is to get professional advice early on in order to secure the most profitable sale. Currently in the UK (where we reside) 'taper relief', an Inland Revenue allowance, makes selling an attractive option. Taper relief reduces the chargeable gain according to how long you held the asset before you disposed of it. The relief is given after all other relief and allowances. The amount of the reduction depends on how long you held the asset (the qualifying holding period) and whether the asset was a business asset or a non-business asset. Taper relief creates a significant argument for entrepreneurs to make money through capital gain rather than through ongoing profits.

UK – taper relief on business assets on or after 6th April 2002	
Number of whole years in the qualifying holding period. This is from the date on which you acquired the asset, or 6th April 1998	Gain remaining chargeable %
Less than 1 year	100
1 year	50
2 years or more	25

Based on tax rates at the time of writing the above could mean paying only 10% tax on any capital gain made, but please refer to your professional tax advisor before making an assumption, as taper relief is not always as straightforward as it first seems.

In particular, on structured deals the Revenue will typically try to charge capital gains on expected sale proceeds rather than just achieved proceeds. It can with taper relief actually make sense to agree payments in advance by way of buying tax credits. This ensures you get your full taper relief on the proceeds and if it turns out you have overpaid the Revenue will repay you.

Tax and elevator deals

Deal structures are complex so there are no rules. However, because the seller is staying on in the business the Revenue can be suspicious. As such, getting taper relief on any assets sold now, whilst extremely likely, has to be handled VERY carefully.

Financial assistance

It should be noted that any deal where the target company offers security over its own assets to secure the borrowing of the purchaser, where that borrowing has been obtained in order to fund the purchaser's acquisition of the target, triggers what is known as 'financial assistance'. Section 151 in the UK Companies Act 1985 prohibits a company from giving financial assistance for the purchase of its own shares and as such specialist legal advice should always be taken in this area.

Deal structure guide summary

In summary, how likely is the seller going to be to receive any future payments? Are the targets that trigger the future payment likely to be met, and if they are will the payment be made? Consider the worst case scenario. What if you only receive the up front payment? It's a judgement of risk versus potential future return.

The sale process – a summary

Once you have prepared for the sale, the process, which is best handled for you by your professional advisors, is as follows:

1. Create a sales information memorandum

Produce two memorandums; an initial short, highly confidential door opener, and a further detailed prospectus. Note: confidentiality is not so important for retail premises of dependent businesses. The detailed prospectus will identify the benefits and saleable features of your business. The presentation of this document, layout, approach and content is crucial in influencing buyers at an early stage. Included should be an overview of the business, its staff, market place, assets, financial position and future potential. Retain commercially sensitive information, such as staff names and key customers until the last moment near completion. This is your goodwill.

If you are a sizeable business, pre-empt buyers' due-diligence requests and create a data room of the likely information that they will want to see.

2. Identifying purchasers

Research and market for potential acquirers; ideally, seek a strategic match where the buyer can obtain economies of scale and synergy from your business. Think laterally. Here a professional broker can prove invaluable, as they will have a comprehensive live database and research facilities to hand. The key is to generate sufficient interest to negotiate the 'most profitable' deal.

3. Confidentiality

For commercial businesses, it is important in the early stages to ensure absolute confidentiality. This is best achieved by disclosing neither the identity nor location of the business in initial discussions. A confidentiality agreement, signed by an interested party, can then be obtained only after the party's seriousness and ability has been obtained.

Sellers should note that confidentially agreements tell trustworthy, honest people the rules. A minority though can't take them seriously, even if signed. Taking an action on them is very difficult, time consuming, hard to prove and expensive. It is therefore a good idea to have a contingency plan such as a cover if there is a leak. For example, admit that you have considered seeking a strategic alliance. Or be ready to point blank refute it.

(For illustrative purposes an example confidentiality undertaking is provided at the back of this book.)

4. Establish buyer's covenant

Establish the buyer's financial position early on. Vet the buyer; if you can't see how they are going to finance it, ask them. Many buyer's will take umbrage at this, so you and your advisers may have to take a view; however, certainly if the buyer makes an offer and especially if they are asking for exclusivity (the opportunity to complete without competition) you must have at least indications. A letter from their accountants, bank statements, or an offer of finance letter ideally. In the case of a PLC buying this is obviously easier. You will know the situation of the company and their latest accounts are public domain.

5. Encourage and influence buyers

If you (and your advisors) have done your job right preparing the business, when you meet the right buyer your business should sell itself. Buyers will want to meet you several times before offering. We believe it is not possible to persuade someone to buy a business, however we believe you can influence greatly. You can only influence by listening first so it is crucial to get buyers to talk. You can influence in the way you present yourself, your business and in follow up meetings it is crucial to be attentive of their needs and do what you can to deliver. Here again a good professional advisor will lead the discussions and assist you with advice at every step.

6. Create a competitive environment

Research and market to find more than one willing and able party; ideally strategic buyers with 'we want/we need' motivation. Ones who will place a high value on your business due to the strategic fit with their plans, and the cost savings and synergies they can achieve. Create a discrete competitive environment (auction) inviting offers. Be careful about hardball playing off; many buyers will simply walk away especially if your business is not unique.

7. Negotiate and agree

Carefully approaching the discussions with a clear appreciation of all parties' objectives. Understand different negotiation tactics and sale structures and keep your objectives in mind. Secure a transaction with the best buyer. Look at the overall picture. It may not be the highest bid, but the securest one in terms of structure and likelihood to complete. Get the offer clearly and in detail in writing.

A good advisor will negotiate the terms for you and use their experience to ensure the nitty gritty does not trip you up. They will create a summary and put into a heads of terms. This is non-legally binding (save in respect of exclusivity and confidentiality). The document outsets the understandings between the parties, prior to producing a definitive legal agreement. Some sellers or buyers like to get their lawyers in at the heads of terms stage, which is understandable, but be aware it is not the sale contract, but a commercial intent. It could take the lawyers as long to agree the principles as to agree the contract.

If in any doubt about the buyer insist that you will not give exclusivity (a clear non-competitive run to completion) unless they can provide comfort. Continue discussions with other parties, even if you accept the offer. Remember, it is not over until the cash is in your account.

(For illustrative purposes an example heads of terms is provided at the back of this book.)

8. Due diligence

Some due diligence may have been undertaken prior to the offer being made and accepted, however once a transaction is agreed, this is where it begins in earnest. Due diligence is, as we have said before, the thorough investigation of the business to ensure the strength of the business.

It will involve the purchaser reviewing commercial aspects such as contracts, staff and key customers. It also involves their solicitors looking at legal issues and their accountants at financial considerations. Some matters may be too commercially sensitive to risk disclosure until negotiations are well advanced.

Due diligence will also drive the sale contract, in particular the warranties and indemnities that the seller will have to give to provide comfort to the buyer about the strength of their business. Once due diligence has been satisfactorily completed legal contracts can be finalized to include protection against any issues highlighted. There may also need to be a review of the price and initial terms agreed if the due diligence has justifiably shown adverse results, or any 'skeletons in the cupboard'.

Whilst an intermediary will help you at every step, the due diligence process is stressful. Unless you have employees such as a Financial Director who can help, you will be burning the midnight oil. There is a lot of paperwork and time involved.

9. Managing the legal team

Buyers and sellers often believe that once they have agreed the deal their lawyers can take care of everything. This is not correct. The lawyers have to work through the documentation carefully and decisions need to be made throughout the process. In particular a large part of the negotiations to form a definitive sale contract will focus on the warranties and indemnities (guarantees) of the seller. The seller should request from the buyer the legal paperwork at an early stage to ensure the buyer is being reasonable on the warranties they are requesting.

As legal negotiations can be complex both buyer and seller should secure the best possible legal advice early on. Appoint a law firm who understands your industry and has the experience and resources to complete the process. When negotiating fees there is a careful balance to maintain. On the one hand you want to be sure of paying the market rate. On the other hand value for money is more than just accepting the lowest price. Quality can justify a premium. Working with your intermediary, choose a legal adviser who:

- specializes in the legal aspects of buying and selling companies
- offers competitive yet effective services and fees
- is able to commit an experienced Partner with the time and resources to lead the deal.

10. Sales contract

This is the final definitive sale document. Once it is signed and the monies are transferred, completion occurs. A large part of this contract will be the warranties and indemnities. A warranty is an undertaking or guarantee offered against a potential event or claim. An indemnity is a final consideration determined or undetermined against a particular or general warranties. Often money will be held in an account (see escrow) against a financial claim being made against a warranty.

As a seller, your and your legal team's job will be to try and limit the warranties both in content and duration. There is no point in achieving a large cash sum, only to have to give it back in a future claim. The seller, of course, will attempt to take a belt and braces approach and get everything they can covered. The parties should work together with their lawyers taking reasonable commercial decisions. There should be compromise on both sides to obtain a final document that is acceptable and not over the top and lengthy for your size of transaction. It will be a complex, stressful and lengthy process to produce this contract. You and your advisors will have invested a lot of time to reach this stage.

In the sale contract, sellers will understandably be expected to provide the buyers a non-compete clause. That is an undertaking to the buyer that they will not set up again and compete with the buyer in a jurisdiction, or period of time. The periods and jurisdiction will depend on the type of business and which country the business is being sold in. It is unlikely to be for more than three years, as most countries recognize it is unfair to restrict someone for an indefinite period from carrying out their trade, and having therefore a livelihood.

There may be other contracts to agree, for example the granting or assignment of lease, or ongoing consultancy contracts for you if it is intended that you will be staying with the transaction.

11. The sale

With good preparation, time and effort invested, and the right advisors, you should achieve a sale. More importantly, through good negotiation and planning, the sale should be one that is profitable, tax effective and rewarding.

Where next?

Now you know how much your business is or could be worth, and how to sell it, should you sell? We examined aspects of this in depth early on in the book in Chapter 3. This is because we believe this question should be answered very early on in a business and owner/manager plan. We believe if the timing is right a sale can be an exciting prelude to new possibilities.

A sale should not however be taken lightly. The timing should be right and in particular a clear idea of what to do next is useful. Without this many business owners, even if the timing is right, fail to let go of their businesses because they have no idea what to do next.

Business owners often get so tied up in day-to-day survival they can forget to ask what they really want out of life. Even when they do get the odd moment to think it is often not objective. There are distractions and emotions that remove this objectivity. Typically these might include, other people's needs, fear of change, greed, fear of getting it wrong, or inability to let go.

Selling a business is different than selling any other asset one owns, because a business is more than an earning asset. It is a lifestyle as well. Therefore, the decision to part with it can be emotional. Personal ambitions should be weighed against economic consequences to achieve a properly balanced decision to sell or not to sell. An ideal time might be when:

- Tax regime favourable on capital gains tax
- Buyers are active
- Cost of capital, interest rates are low
- Your profit level with current market multiples satisfy your capital gain goal
- Your business still offers buyers growth
- Your lifestyle goals are met
- You know roughly what you want to do next

There may also be reasons to sell:

- Retirement or ill health
- Stress
- A partner or major shareholder seeking a return on their stake
- Boredom
- Competitive/red tape pressures
- Frustrated
- Lack of second tier management
- Undercapitalized venture

Should you take an offer and quit while you are ahead? Well, if you are made an offer you cannot refuse but satisfies your goals, we say take it. The world is full of people who hold out for the last penny and then miss the boat. We have lost count for example of the number of 70 plus year olds (particularly men) who can't let go, yet they are losing touch with their business and relying on a health which although often surprisingly robust can decline rapidly. Enjoy it whilst you have got it, we say. Okay we know you enjoy your business and are frightened of being bored, but there must be other things you can do. You don't have to do the shopping every week. You can order it on the net and get it delivered whilst you do what you have always wanted to.

One of the objectives of selling is to get your eggs out of the same basket, create liquid assets and diversify your wealth. No one would ever sell a business unless they have a reason to sell it. If you are bored, frustrated, worried about your health, near retirement (or well over it) or undercapitalized than sell it and move on. The more established your business is the more secure it is, but remember no business ever becomes totally secure. Shares can go up as well as down.

Take the time out to think objectively about your and your family's needs. It may be the right time to sell. You may have a good reason to sell. It may be right to stay. You have bought choice and the freedom to exercise it. Plan and imagine the possibilities without fear.

REALITY CHEQUE

ELECTRO-MECHANICAL ENGINEERING **SOUTH ENGLAND**
T/O £2.1M **JULY 2003**

It's one of life's truisms that seemingly small decisions can change your life forever. For Alan Peel that decision was almost thirty years ago when, as an oil and gas adviser to a large PLC, he placed a contract with a newly formed electro-mechanical engineering firm. It was the first big contract the firm had been awarded and a friendship was formed between Alan and the MD that would change Alan's life.

For twenty years Alan worked as a consultant in the offshore oil and gas industry advising companies such as BP and Shell on methods of bringing gas and oil on shore. Although perfectly happy in his work Alan had always dreamt of owning his own business. Which is why when his friend told him that he was retiring and selling his electro-mechanical engineering firm Alan decided to buy the company he had given that first contract to.

The business designed, manufactured and supplied equipment and materials for the oil, gas, marine and petrochemical industries. A fully qualified workforce undertook all the installation, testing and commissioning services. What distinguished this business from many of their competitors was that they were approved suppliers to the leading oil and gas operating companies and had long-established relationships with distributors, agencies and overseas customers. In fact 80% of the work was in the Middle East.

After six years of running the company Alan began to carefully consider his future. He took professional advice and began to plan his exit route. Alan felt that it was better to sell the business when there was no pressing urgency, while he was relatively young and in good health. In addition, he had begun to feel that his responsibilities as Managing Director were becoming too onerous and that his workload was not leaving him enough time to enjoy the fruits of his labours.

Avondale began marketing the company in December 2001 and within six months three potential purchasers had met Alan to discuss a possible transaction. Alan accepted an offer through Avondale in July 2003.

Alan is now enjoying semi-retirement, although he does undertake some consultancy work to keep his hand in. And he still keeps in touch with the friend who helped him achieve his ambition.

"Art is making something out of nothing and selling it."
Frank Zappa

chapter eleven Negotiate to win – Your money or your life!

ELEVEN Negotiate to win – Your money or your life!

"An investment in knowledge always pays the best interest."
Benjamin Franklin

"Am I not destroying my enemies when I make friends of them?"
Abraham Lincoln

"Drawing on my fine command of the language, I said nothing."
Robert Benchley

Chapter focus

We explain the negotiation process in a business buy and sell situation, pointing out some of the options that can be built into a deal. We also cover specific techniques to use and guard against from both buyer and seller standpoints.

- **Introduction**
- **Negotiation game play**
- **Setting your strategy**
- **Objectives, yours and theirs**
- **Influencing versus persuasion**
- **Building rapport**
- **Strategic moves**
- **Strategic moves explored**
- **Summary**

Introduction

The capital gain you make from the sale of your business will be the difference between the price you pay to buy the business, or the start-up capital you inject, and what you eventually negotiate at sale completion. This difference will have taken a lot of hard work from you adding value at every step. At sale time you ideally want every penny, and strong negotiation skills is the key to this.

As we mentioned in our valuation chapter, ultimately a business is worth what someone will pay for it on the open market. This means your negotiation skills can have a big impact on your capital gain. Buy low, sell high and you win. In this chapter we will look at the negotiation process and also cover some of the technical negotiations involved in a business sale or purchase. In this chapter we will look at specific tactics to both use and be aware of in the negotiation of a business sale. We look from the perspective of both the buyer and seller, which is in itself a necessary technique, whichever role you are playing!

As with much of this book, negotiation is a subject to itself and there are many excellent detailed books available. Consequently whilst we aim to provide some tips, strategy and ideas we also recommend further reading on the subject.

Negotiation game play

Many people don't enjoy haggling. In part this depends on where you were raised. In Britain there is a culture of seeing it as rude. In India, it is the way of all business transactions, and seen as an essential and fun part of life. If you are going to be in business you need to adopt the Indian philosophy. If you do find negotiation stressful it will go against you. Negotiation is a game so enjoy it. Okay, if you are buying or selling a business it is a very important game and one you need to win. Like any game, having a good strategy, understanding of the rules and coach will help your play immensely. So will being able to appreciate and anticipate the other player's moves.

We compare business negotiation to chess and poker. If you have not played these games or learnt them, now is your excuse. We liken it to chess because this game is all about understanding your resources (pieces), the possible moves that can be made and calculating which ones to use and when. In chess, the more steps you can successfully compute ahead, both in respect of your own moves and in anticipation of the other player's moves, the more likely your chance of success. So it is again with negotiation, although like chess, be wary of being too smart – you can get so wrapped up in thinking ahead and in your own moves, you miss the obvious simple ones being made by the other player in front of you. In chess and business negotiation you need to:

- Think ahead
- Understand and anticipate other player's moves and strategy
- Re-computing your strategy and analyzing theirs every time the other player makes a move
- Taking time to step back and think
- Understand the resources available to you
- Have a game plan in advance and adapt it to an advantage as you progress
- Practice
- Have a good experienced coach.

So, chess grandmasters can make really good negotiators, but why is a card game like poker similar to business negotiation? Poker, as business negotiation, is a game of chance but you can increase the odds in your favour, predominantly by understanding how the other players will react and assessing this quickly. In poker, being able to anticipate who will call a bluff or being able to hold a bluff with a straight face is vital. Even choosing to play the odd bluff takes guts, particularly when the sums are large. Additionally, understanding what level you can push the game to maximize the bet without everyone folding too early when you have a good hand is again vital. Even understanding what is a good hand is important. In poker and business negotiation you need to:

- Have the guts to bluff sometimes and with a straight face
- Know when you are being bluffed
- Quickly judge the style of other players and therefore their moves
- Re-computing your strategy and analyzing theirs every time the other player makes a move
- Be able to quickly calculate the strength of your hand and the odds of a win
- Knowing when to fold (give in) and when not to
- Take time to step back and think

- Be able to stand the pressure of betting or gambling
- Choose what level to pitch your bets or value at
- Practice
- Have a good coach.

We have used gaming as a comparison for one final reason. Many people see negotiation as adversarial. They use words like 'my argument' and they see it as their job to win their needs over their opponent. Yes we want to win, but does it matter? Indeed, is it not better if the other player wins as well? That is why 'player' is a better word than 'opponent', which suggests conflict. A game is also after all supposed to be a sport and we believe is best handled with a sporting code of conduct. Great negotiators will seek win/wins where both sides are happy. Win/wins are usually faster and easier.

Gaining the power to negotiate

Prior to undertaking negotiation we believe it is important to have an understanding of your position and power to negotiate. We have already discussed that many people don't like negotiation. This is partly because of a fear of failure but if you examine the resources available to you we hope that it will give you more confidence and understanding of your power to negotiate. We believe there are six main aspects that give you this power:

1. Your character

Understanding who you are and how others see you is vital in successful negotiation. To be a successful negotiator the more you can get people to follow you and lead, the better you will be as a negotiator. We examine leadership in Chapter 11 so this is essential reading for gaining the power to negotiate.

A quick summary of essential characteristics might include listening, saying thank-you, humour, dramatizing ideas, caring about others, adopting humility, being passionate, excellent communication and influencing and persuading people.

Finally, be positive. Don't judge people and their points of view. Avoid closed words like issue, bad, wrong. Approach everything with a 'never say never' attitude. Remember, there is no territory, so keep high emotion, anger and tenseness away from the deal table.

2. Your job title

Although we don't believe your job position should have a significant bearing in your power to negotiate if you have all the other skills, if your business card says you have power people assume you do, and you should react accordingly.

3. Skills

Negotiation is a skill and can be learnt. There are many techniques. The more you practice and study it the greater your awareness of what works and does not work. Which is the right move and when? The faster you can move, the easier it becomes. Don't just see negotiation as a business skill; make it a hobby. Even when you negotiate with your kids on the weekend over whether they are allowed an ice cream or not, see if you can outplay them by thinking further ahead and using a move (tactics of confusion/distraction?). Give yourself a score for a successful win.

4. Planning and strategy

Fortune favours the prepared man. Planning is vital to your success. Taking the time to think about your strategy and game play well in advance will give you power and avoid catching you by surprise. The better your strategy the more likely you are to achieve your objectives. See below.

5. Information

Knowledge is power, as they say. The more understanding you have about the strengths and weaknesses of the other player then the greater manoeuvrability you have. If you know where the Achilles heel is you can push at it. What you need to avoid is your nice thought-out case or strategy being broadsided early on by a fact you were not aware about. Have the correct facts and figures to support your case.

It is prudent to assume that everybody and every business has 'skeletons in the cupboard' somewhere. The other player is going to emphasize what he sees as the strongest points. He won't necessarily tell lies, but is it the whole truth? A good negotiator would even bring them out early on and deal with them.

Alternatively, understanding how someone else might value what you have and being able to play to this will increase the value you receive.

Buyers will carry out due diligence to get information, but sellers should conduct due diligence on their prospective buyers. Don't assume that they have the money to make a purchase or the ability to close the deal; ask for evidence.

6. Your natural game play and instinct

As you develop as a negotiator your confidence will grow. We believe that experience will develop instinct. Instinct is important, it comes from the gut. How does the situation feel? What feels like the right move?

By understanding the attributes that give you power, you can develop your power; initially it will be a conscious effort, eventually it will become sub-conscious. But remember, never overestimate your ability and never underestimate the other players.

Setting your strategy

The most prepared players think ahead. We believe that it helps to think of negotiation and its planning in stages. Depending on the negotiation there may be 100s, but we have produced 10 steps to help you with your planning.

Stage	Action
1	Set out your objectives and review the big picture
2	Create a plan (make sure you have an alternative worst case plan)
3	Explore the culture of the deal (people, approach, market perception)
4	Identify needs and interest of all parties
5	Analyze offer options, establish an offer and contingency offer
6	Present offer in best style (writing/verbal depends on situation)
7	Bargain, discuss, influence and persuade (step back and think if needs be)
8	Secure commitment from the party and get it in writing for clarity
9	Undertake next step (instruct lawyers, accountants etc?)
10	Examine success (or failures) and learn from experience

Objectives; yours and theirs

To negotiate well you have to take three perspectives: yours, theirs and as a fly on the wall (third party) looking at the big picture. These different perspectives will help you to see things from different points of view. This is known as positioning. If you can think like the other party you can manoeuvre them to where you want. Don't forget, if they are any good they will be doing the same (never underestimate your opponent).

Positioning enables you to make your moves not just coming from what you want, but also taking into account how the other party are likely to react. Alex's book *'Advanced Selling for Beginners'* goes into this in more depth.

People see things differently and understanding this is crucial to being a good negotiator, after all negotiation is about successfully bridging the gap between your needs and theirs. A good negotiator will establish early on the top priorities of the other party. It may be speed not price for example. Ask people straight what their top priorities are on doing a deal. Whatever they respond with will be valuable information to you.

Your thinking needs to be in time, if not in line, with that of the other party. In other words, put yourself in their shoes. It is not good enough to just understand their position or to examine what you would do in their position. You have to actually try imagining how they might think. Incidentally, this is very hard and involves really understanding other people, so being a student of human nature really helps in negotiation. Oh, and by the way, whilst you are trying to get in the zone of how the other player thinks don't forget your objectives.

Influencing versus persuasion

Why is this understanding of different perspectives, needs and information so crucial? Aristotle summed it up brilliantly some 2500 years ago.

"The fool tells me his reasons; the wise man persuades me with my own."

This phrase is crucial. Many people think that good negotiators are hardball tough cookies, people that don't budge, or are stubborn. In fact the opposite is true: top negotiators get things moving and make it possible by creating a win/win environment where both sides are happy, and the parties don't feel persuaded, more that they have been influenced. Usually this requires compromise from both sides.

The Oxford Popular Dictionary definition uses the following words to describe persuasive, *to coax, cajole, and convince*. For influencing it uses, *to effect, guide, direct, lead and motivate*. There is a fundamental difference, and essentially our contention is that the best negotiators can do both, probably ultimately influencing more than persuading. We also believe the same applies to sales. Essentially the premise is that more informed buyers, which we all are in the information age, will make their own mind up. Therefore, the sales man or negotiator's job is to 'help' the prospect (or in negotiation the other player) make their mind up freely in your favour. This is known as consultative selling or negotiation.

Building rapport

We have already examined that your character has a significant effect on your power to negotiate. Our contention is that if great negotiators need to influence, not persuade, then they need to be liked and trusted. We believe it is possible to use some basic techniques to systematically build this trust, or rapport. We can't make you likeable (you may not be); however, what we can do is suggest techniques that help make you likeable! These include:

- Listening
- Showing respect for the other player
- Relating to the other player's needs and genuinely going out of your way to understand them
- Showing an interest in the other player and what they enjoy
- Paying attention and really caring about the other player's needs (even if you can't meet them)
- Showing you care (often missed)
- Mirroring (reflecting) their style. For example, if they like talking things over, then talk them over. Don't insist they put it in writing. You can do this afterwards
- Mirroring their character/interests. If you have a keen golfer, don't over-talk them all the time and invite them to Motor-sport. Actually they might like this also, but you get the idea
- Using open body language, such as open arm posture (not crossed)

- Ensuring that negotiation venues are thought out for the needs of the other player (as well as yours). Should the meeting be on their turf for example, where they will feel more comfortable?
- Avoiding adversarial seating. Putting yourself directly at the head or opposite (round tables are good for avoiding this)

Buying or selling, we all prefer to deal with someone that we like and trust. People do business with people in the end. If we like the 'other side' we will have a natural rapport and want to do business with them. When we trust them we stop worrying if we got the best deal possible or if there is something important that we missed.

Obtaining rapport therefore is crucial to your success in negotiation. If you are on the other side of these techniques, go with it. It will make the negotiation game easier and less stressful; however have your eyes and ears open the whole time and see past the rapport and charm to whether what is being offered really meets your needs. You can still say 'no' to someone you get on with.

Whilst we recommend we all go out with a likeable rapport-building approach, there is a cautionary comment. Lying is something that you have to be aware of. Most people, if they catch somebody lying once, will never trust anything else they ever say. We always assume that there is something that they are not telling us. People actually give themselves away through their body language and/or tone of voice if they are lying. The only exception is when they actually believe the lie themselves or they have exceedingly well developed acting skills. You have to know though how to read the signals. I would suggest that you are wary of interpreting mannerisms and look them in the eye as you ask questions like:

- What do you want to sell?
- What is the one thing you least want me to find out?
- What is the weakest aspect of your business?
- What will you do if you don't sell it?
- Have you got anybody else actively interested at the moment?
- How long have you been interested in selling?

A final comment on rapport and relationships: ego can be a valuable asset in a negotiation, theirs not yours that is. Yours is a liability. Good negotiators play upon the other person's ego and self-esteem.

Strategic moves

We have already discussed that negotiation is a game. A very important one and like any game there are many moves, tactics and strategies. Understanding them, using them and spotting them are crucial in negotiation. Imagine you are a judge in a chess game, if you can hold objectivity (a judge is third party) even when a good move is played on you, appreciate it for its beauty and strategy, you will then transcend the moves and be able to concentrate on defending them and your game plan. Let's face it, does it matter what moves are played so long as you meet your ultimate objectives?

There are too many moves to list in this book but here, from our experience, are common ones, not listed in any particular order, with our recommended defence. Employing an intermediary will assist you in negotiations, as a good advisor will know and be able to apply in a practiced manner most of the moves. Ultimately they are therefore the best defence against the moves.

Move	Explanation	Defence
Red herring	Pretending to be interested in one thing but actually have their interest in another area, "We are concerned about the management…"	Ignore the herring and spot the real issue
Tactics of confusion	Using jargon, requesting reams of information, attacking the parties, charming then complaining. Leaves the other player reeling, uncertain and confused to undermine confidence.	Similar to red herring. Spot it, and then ignore it and concentrate on the issues and what you want.
Good cop, bad cop	Two people who are really one team, approaching you in a different way to confuse you and open you up.	Treat each equally and look past their approach at what they are really saying.
Low value concessions for big value ones	A concession gives what can amount to the illusion of making a compromise. This in turn encourages one. Deliberately give small concessions and make them seem big, and demand big concessions in return.	Spot them and return a small concession with smaller concessions, or not at all. Remember, six small concessions can be less than half as much as one big one, but you can give the impression of making compromises all the way.

Move	Explanation	Defence
Walking away	Sometimes you need to be firm (or feign it to gain advantage). It is not enough to pick up your coat to walk out. People do business with those they trust and have a good rapport with, so be non-adversarial. Being a gentleman or lady does not mean that you cannot play hard. Don't look back unless of course the other player calls your bluff (if it was one).	Accept it but suggest the door is still open giving the other player the ability to come back without loosing pride.
Third party referrals tactic	A good way of saying no without it being your fault thus maintaining a good relationship. Often used to justify a fixed position, "My accountant says it's worth X maximum ..."	Ignore it and talk directly to your player putting your position in. Don't attempt to argue with the justification.
Conditional concession	If I... Would you...? The conditional concession dangles a carrot in front of you; if done skilfully, one that they have found motivates you. It is safe by testing the water on your response before they make the concession whilst seeming very reasonable.	Is the concession being offered equivalent to the one being asked for? If not then offer a different one, or not one at all.
Leverage (pressure or power points)	This is not so much a move as it is a fundamental of negotiation. Essentially it is where you exert a particular requirement with a significant influencer in order to direct or influence the other party to react in your favour. For example, securing or bluffing that you have more than one buyer (you should) in order to create fear of loss to secure commitment from uncertain party. Or having a significantly expandable business with demonstrable proof to back this case up. Make a list of your leverage points and use them.	Leverage points are essential in negotiation. Most people are aware of them, although they don't use them as systematically as they could. Many are hugely influencing or persuasive and as such are best put gently to the other player, as the other player can feel forced if they are over-exerted. The defence is to examine the true strength of the leverage and spot weakness, or hold back with equal leverage point.

Move	Explanation	Defence
Trust me	It is a move played but not one we approve of. Indeed, players that say this normally have the opposite in mind.	We suggest that you trust everyone without giving him or her an opportunity to prove themselves to be less than trustworthy.
What if? The hypothetical fireside chats	Relax the other side and start vaguely (but in a planned way) and explore the possibilities? This tests the ground and should gain you valuable information about the other side, without you putting any formal commitment forward on your part.	Either don't respond, or be very careful with your answers. A chat is never just a chat when playing this game, no matter what anyone says.
Time deadlines	Putting in deadlines (often false) can panic players into making hasty decisions with you pressurizing them in your favour.	Ask if it is a real deadline. Why is it real? If it does not seem real ignore it. Be careful if you play a false deadline and your bluff is called – it can make you look silly. What if you then have a real one later?
Shock opening bid	Giving powerful false objections to a business at the time of offer to validate a reason for a significantly lower shocking offer with the aim of undermining the seller's confidence and throw them off balance.	The objections are not real. Handle them and you validate them, so do so at your peril. Feel good that you have a tangible offer, then concentrate on the price and simply say 'not enough'.
False justifications data	The politician's favourite to negotiate a win with their voters. You can manipulate data to say pretty much anything to justify your case.	Listen to the justification. Check the data and the manipulations. Don't argue, just beg to differ.
Fait accompli	Talk as though the deal has already been done, and keep talking as though the deal has already been done. Sales professionals call this the assumptive close. You believe so much it is going to happen, others fall in behind.	Fall in behind IF it is in your interest.

Move	Explanation	Defence
Silence	Brilliant move and massively under utilized, particularly in verbal discussions. Most people can't stand silence so when you make a move follow it with silence and shut up. The other player will normally fill the gap and show their cards in the process. As the old saying goes 'he who speaks first normally loses'.	Mirror it with equal silence. Silence is peaceful, it can't hurt anyone. We recommend just counting in your head to see how long it goes. Two real players will smile after about a minute as they both spot they have been spotted, then move on. Or if you really can't take the silence and you want to buy time to think, make a vague comment and excuse. "Hmmm. Interesting. Can I nip to the toilet just for a second." Now you have time to think. Think fast, what is your next move?
Playing hard to get	Similar to silence, feigning lack of interest to undermine the other party's confidence.	Keep smiling and firmly state position.
Timing	This is not so much a move but also how the moves are executed. For example, say yes too quickly and easily to an offer and a buyer may feel you agreed too fast and they could have got it for less. Result they chip away at the price later on. Allow people time to think over what you have said; like a meal, ideas need digesting.	Be conscious of your pace and try and play it at an even pace. If you are impatient or hasty by nature recognize this and ask for help from others to hold you back before you open discussions.
Make me an offer	This is best done when no price or offering is provided. The move places the other player under pressure to work out what they want without knowing what you want. It also allows the market to decide ultimately the value of something, particularly if it is carried out in an auction style.	Avoid it if you can by asking questions. The old rule is 'he who speaks first loses', so try and gain an impression if you can from the other player by asking indirect questions or hypothetical questions 'off the record'. Real players may still say nothing so go for it, be vague and give yourself lots of room to manoeuvre on your first offer once you start gauging their reaction.

Move	Explanation	Defence
Chip away	Agreeing high terms to secure the other player's commitment (preferably with exclusivity or a lock-in). For example, the other player is excluded from negotiation with someone else for a period of time. Then once you have a lock-in find little justifications to chip at the price.	Recognize whether they are genuine justifications for a chip away or deliberate moves just to get you up or down.
Last minute reduction	Line everything up and get everything agreed. Take it to the last minute and then come up with false objections/ justification to create last minute increase or decrease.	Spot it for what it is, a bluff. Examine the strength of your position (other options etc) and then call the bluff by walking away. It should be a bluff, but there is no guarantee!
Base square to final square	Moving the other player early on with such haste to the final point (square) they let their defences down and give away on key points. For example: "If I pay you all cash and close quickly, what's the least you would accept?"	Answer this move and you are dead. If it is played on you, smile and say 'nice try'.
Moving the goalposts	Changing the terms of the deal to your advantage, usually with a false justification, or 'selective memory'.	Get it in writing. Get it in writing. Get it in writing. Got it?
Selective memory	A lot of our defences have been to ignore the move once you spot them. This is similar, you simply select the bits on offer you like and try and dismiss the bits you don't like	Same as moving goal posts, get it in writing.
Go direct	Intermediaries know the game and the moves, so it can make sense to undermine them and go direct to the other player. They may be less experienced than the adviser. If you complain about the adviser you may even be able to undermine the other player's confidence in them.	A bit of a cynical tactic but the defence is spotting it when it is being undertaken. Remember that the other player is trying to gain. If you have chosen well your adviser will be competent and be there to help you by creating a buffer to such cynical players. Players executing this move should be aware that it could backfire due to lack of nobility in approach leading to poor trust.

Move	Explanation	Defence
Breaking deadlock move	This is actually a positive move that normally helps both parties. When a deadlock or deteriorating situation is reached, create time for all to reflect. Deadlocks should be approached with a positive 'where there is a will there is a way' approach. Deadlocks normally result from channel thinking. If it isn't working take a whole different approach. All players should brainstorm no matter how wacky the ideas (some wacky ideas usually turn out to be good ones).	Encourage it, it helps both parties.
The Colombo	After the American TV detective who lulled people into believing he was a lot less capable than they were. Playing dumb or hustling. Letting the opponent deliberately underestimate your skills.	Spot it and be ready for the next move; don't let it catch you by surprise.
Final offer	By stating something is a final offer, strongly discourages counter offers. It is easy afterwards to change your mind. Be careful though, use it too often and no one will be convinced. Sometimes of course in every deal it will really be a final offer.	Ignore the comment. Carry on and counter-move anyway.
Pre-empt	Essentially this move is a counter to a move that you can see the other player is likely to make before they even get there. For example, you may anticipate the other player will insist on a fast deal. If you can't deliver this, manage their expectations before they insist.	You don't always have to listen. It may be time for selective memory.
Surprise	Deliberately planning to catch people on the hop. The surprise visit or telephone call. Catch people when they are not expecting it and their guard is down.	Access your position? Are you off guard? If so, buy time with a delay.

Strategic moves explored

All these moves are being detailed in isolation but great players will run them simultaneously and in a planned and co-ordinated manner. It is worth noting that some players carry out these moves naturally without even noticing they do it. I am sure those of you with children will recognize the charm move when your kids want something.

It should be noted that all the defences depend on the strength of your position. It should also be noted that whilst most of these moves are put forward as bluffs (that is feigned moves), there is no guarantee they are. Yours and your adviser's job is to try and work out which one's are if they are being played on you. For example, we have known shock opening bids to be genuine bids with genuine objections where the buyer just does not value the business at any more. If they are the only buyer then it may not be such a daft offer after all.

Make a study of the other player before deciding which moves to make. People and circumstances are different, so many moves that worked on your last game will be hopeless against this player. Be flexible in your approach; different people react differently.

One last thought on your strategic moves: if buying and selling is a game, the more you plan and think ahead the more you are likely to win your objectives. This means it is vital to take time out, think and plan. You can do deals quickly but you should still spend a lot of time on it to make sure it is done correctly and all the aspects have been thought out. If you can't find time to plan, then buy time. Some good time buyers are:

- No, not yet.
- Can't speak at the moment. Can I call you back?
- Holidays (under-utilized in our opinion). You get time to think objectively and relaxed.
- Third party referral; 'must talk that over with the…'
- Hmmm, interesting, let me think about it (the best one and so simple it's beautiful, also probably the truth).

Summary

There are many highly technical aspects to a business sale or purchase. We cover these in Chapter 10. We have also provided in the appendix we hope some useful resource tools including a heads of terms, deal timetable and confidentiality undertaking. Other tools are available online at www.avondale-group.co.uk.

To summarize, there is a lot involved in negotiation and it requires a significant range of tools and skills, including probably the most difficult, an understanding of human nature. This complexity is why, carried out correctly and successfully, negotiation can be highly satisfactory. Remember, it's not the taking part that counts it's the winning. Good luck.

"The fool tells me his reasons; the wise man persuades me with my own."

Aristotle

chapter twelve In a nutshell

TWELVE In a nutshell

Chapter focus

Bringing together the key points.

There are many books that cover in depth many of the topics we have covered. Our aim was not to provide a definitive expert guide on all aspects, more to provide an insight and perhaps an inspiration into the role of the owner/manager and how we firmly believe building and selling a business can provide both time and capital wealth.

We know it is rare for a business book to cover both technical business aspects and personal considerations around life goals. Having written the book we know why; it's hard. We believe there is another reason it's rare, and it is simply that most business advisors like to ignore the truth that it is people that make businesses real. Quality systems, technical knowledge, finances, brand and skills all have a bearing of course, indeed we have argued much for this in the book. Ultimately however, in the small to medium business market it is people who drive a business and who determine whether it is a successful one. Often this is a new entrepreneur or owner/manager doing their best to drive their business forward. Many professionals seem to ignore that such people do so for their own ends, their own personal goals and their own lifestyle reasons and that these must be examined as part of an overall strategy.

Perhaps we should all start avoiding such expressions as work/life balance or play hard/work hard. It seems to us that by using such terms we are separating the personal from business or work. Who said work cannot be play? Who said there is such a thing as work/life balance? Surely there is only life? By dividing the personal from the business we believe there is a real danger of forgetting that businesses are there to serve the needs of people, both their customers, staff and their owners. Interestingly, in a recent employee survey a majority rated having a best friend at work as one of the greatest reasons for staying put and being loyal to a business.

Has this anything to do with the pay they receive or the success they achieve in their role?

What do you want from life? What do you want from work? In a small to mid-size business, for the owner/manager the two are the same. It may be that building and running a growing enterprise is your thing for a while. It may be for life, or it may be a prelude to a new beginning, especially if you have gained capital wealth from a sale.

Wealth is in limited supply and we are competing for it. To win it, in an increasingly fast moving environment you need competitive advantage. Wealth if measured by accountants would be a sum of all the property, machinery, goodwill etc. Yet the real wealth in businesses today is the ideas and knowledge in people's heads to take it forward. Where you are today is a result of what you thought and took action on in the past. Once you believe this you realize that gaining suitable ideas to build opportunities to start, buy or build a business is a decision you make, rather than something determined outside of you.

Accumulating wealth is the key to financial and time independence, not achieving a high salary. If you look at the salaries of people like Bill Gates and Warren Buffett you will find that there are thousands of people in America with higher salaries, yet there are few with higher wealth. They never focused their financial goals on achieving the highest salary they could. People in large organizations or even small ones get used to seeing status and salary level as the same thing. The way entrepreneurs look at it, the higher your salary the greater factor you have to multiply it to calculate what somebody else is earning off your work.

Our idea is that rather than just working for a living and saving for a pension until you are 65 (or is it 70 now?), or running a business just for income you can do something different. Our idea is that by starting, buying or building a business you can provide both an income, capital wealth and, in time, life wealth. It's not a new idea, there are many people who have already successfully trodden the road, however in today's attractive tax regime (UK), we believe the road is more open. The road is also more open because ideas in a knowledge and service based economy (UK) mean businesses can start up or grow with less capital and move and grow faster. The competitive environment means there are more buyers for smaller companies as everyone is trying to get ahead. The lifestyle choices we all have today are greater.

If you are an existing owner/manager, we hope we have given you some ideas to help you grow your business and maximize its value, or simply tell you how to sell it if you have had enough and want to move on to new pastures. For potential owner/managers we hope we have inspired you to have a go, either through a start-up or buying an existing venture.

The successful owner/manager or would be entrepreneur will spend a lot of time listening, seeking knowledge and advice, thinking and planning. They will then translate these into action through hard work. Some of it will work, some of it won't, but if you carefully manage the risks and get more right than wrong you are in with a good chance of building a business for capital wealth and personal freedom.

Good luck. Ah, now that's a bad sign off. You see we don't believe in luck, just good ideas, working smart and hard. Make a difference.

"Confidence is a state of mind, a state of being which you become."

'Buddha'

"The future belongs to those who believe in the beauty of their dreams."

Eleanor Roosevelt

"The human mind is our fundamental resource."

John Fitzgerald Kennedy

Sample heads of terms

UK Based SME Company

Date:

Ref:

This document outlines the 'head' terms agreed between the parties, prior to negotiation of a final sale and purchase agreement. Save in the respect of confidentiality and exclusivity the terms are not legally binding, and are subject to due diligence and contract.

The parties are ("the Parties")

The Vendor

Name

Address

Postcode

The Purchaser

Name

Address

Postcode

1. The sale basis

Mr and Mrs shareholders/XYZ company *("the Vendor") will sell to Mr & Mrs purchaser/ABC company ("the Purchaser"),* the business *known as* (XYZ name, of 28, XY Street, any town) (or company XYZ reg.no.123456678) *and any associated names ("the Business"). The sale will be on* a fixed asset and goodwill basis/share transfer basis.

2. Timescale

The parties will conduct their best endeavours to secure completion by (date XYZ)

3. Purchase Price/Terms

The purchaser will pay the vendor as follows:			
Item	**Amount**	**Payable**	Note
Initial payment	£	On completion	For the purchase of the entire share capital of the Business to include the net assets at completion to be at least £__________
Retention	£	One month after completion	A payment will be made and held in escrow on completion. This will be released one month after completion after adjustment for any variance in the estimated net asset value or warranty claims.
Deferred payment	£	Repayable by ('XYZ Date')	A deferred payment will be made. This will be paid in 12 equal instalments with the first payment one month after completion. The payments will be plus interest at 2% above base rate.
Performance related payment	£	Repayable by ('XYZ Date')	A performance related payment will be made. This will be paid 12 calendar months from the day of completion at the rate of 25p in the £ on all turnover above £500,000 up to £1,000 000 million. Target £25,000.
Target	£TOTAL		

4. Deferred or performance consideration shall be secured by:

- a personal guarantee will be provided from the Purchaser to the Vendor (if smaller/or new co-acquirer) and
- a charge over the freehold property of the Purchaser OR
- a debenture on the assets of the Company
- the Purchaser providing key-man insurance or life assurance to protect outstanding payments in the eventuality of critical illness or death.

The Company's Act 1985 states that the company shall not assist in its own purchase. Some deal structures or financing requirements of a purchase can constitute such financial assistance which may necessitate a legal and accounting procedure known as a 'white-wash' to be undertaken to still allow the transaction to proceed. The Purchaser agrees that advice in this respect will be sought from their legal advisers early on.

The Purchaser will enter into covenants with the Vendors to preserve the asset value of the Company for as long as any consideration remains outstanding. The Vendor shall remain as a signatory on the Company's bank account until the Deferred Consideration is fully repaid.

5. Premises

The current premises are **XYZ address, anywhere**

Detail property situation and agreement between parties. Lease (and terms of) or freehold, owned individually, or as a company?

6. Consultancy or handover

The Vendor agrees to provide the Purchaser a *2-week* initial handover *free of charge* during office hours. Thereafter, they agree to be available by telephone or fax within reason for a further period of *(six months). OR handover on earnings basis (detail contract terms).*

7. Resignations share deals

The following shall resign as directors on completion... XYZ and ABC exiting directors' names.

8. Employees

Detail any specific agreements, including if an asset deal TUPE (transfer undertaking of protection of employment) situation.

9. Tax

The Parties agree to give fair consideration to each other's tax position in the negotiation of a final sale and purchase agreement. *The following is for asset deals only* The Parties will agree an apportionment of the sale price between *('goodwill, fixed assets and leasehold interest/freehold')* for tax purposes.

10. Non-compete and protection of goodwill

To protect the goodwill the Vendor will provide covenants that they will not for a reasonable period and within reasonable proximity enter into a competitive business or carry out an action that might materially affect the goodwill of the Business. The Vendor will also conduct the Business in its normal and ordinary course until completion.

11. Confidentiality, due diligence and disclosure

The Parties agree that the terms, negotiations and sale are confidential save in taking counsel from their professional advisors, or as required by the rules and regulations of the London Stock Exchange, or any TUPE obligation to consult with employees.

The Parties agree to disclose any facts material to the transaction. The Vendor will grant the Purchaser or their advisors and employees access to the Business, its operations and books in order to perform due diligence. Access will be provided consistent with the Vendor's requirement to protect confidentiality.

12. Representations and warranties

The Vendor agrees to provide and the Purchaser agrees to request warranties, indemnities and representations appropriate for a transaction of this size.

13. Advisor's fees and costs

The Parties agree to instruct early on appropriate advisors to complete a transaction of this size in the timescale proposed. Each party shall be responsible for their own advisor's fees and costs incurred in the transaction.

14. Exclusivity and deposit

The Vendor agrees to provide exclusivity to the Purchaser up to the target date for completion subject to reasonable progress being made by the Purchaser. During such exclusivity the Vendor or their advisors will not before completion discuss, negotiate or provide assistance to any third party who may be interested in the Business. *Reasonable progress may include providing the Vendor's advisers with proof of funding progress. Such exclusivity is subject to the Purchaser paying a deposit of (£) to be held by ( ) on behalf of the Vendor.*

15. Terms

English law will govern these Heads of Terms and the sale and purchase agreement.

____

Vendor's signature **Purchaser's signature**

Date: / /0 Date: / /0

Produced by ______________________________

Contact Details

Email Address ______________________________

Tele No ______________________________

Sample basic confidentiality wording

The below is not a full confidentiality undertaking but demonstrates the type of form of wording that is required.

Terms of undertaking

You are undertaking to treat any information provided as strictly confidential, including ensuring that all reasonable precautions are taken to ensure such confidentiality. In addition you undertake that all information provided will be used only for evaluating the business with a view to acquisition and that at no time will information be disclosed or otherwise made available to any third party, other than to your officers, employees or professional advisors who are required in the course of (and solely for the purpose of such an evaluation) to receive and consider the information and provided that such officers, employees and advisors are aware and accept the strict provisions of this undertaking. You also agree to return if requested, any information provided including in whatever form supplied written, electronic, data storage, etc.

This undertaking is to be governed and construed in accordance with English Law. You are undertaking that you have read, understood and agreed to the terms upon which additional information will be provided and that you understand any breach of these terms will be vigorously pursued.

Sample initial information shortlist

- **Staff Schedule**
- **Inventory of fixed assets**
- **Product details**
- **Market Overview**
- **Property Details**
- **Year-end Accounts (certified/audited)**
- **Management accounts**

Sample pre-due diligence questionnaire

Section	Item	Put enclosures or detail notes	✔
Accounts	Please supply the latest copies of your accounts. Management accounts and/or VAT returns since the last accounting date.		
Property	Please provide a plan of the property occupied by the business to be shown edged in red. Please provide a copy of your lease. Are there any boundary disputes, disputes with your neighbours or planning disputes? Are there any local authority proposals that may affect your business? Are there any rights of access over your property?	 Yes / No – If yes, please give details. Yes / No – If yes, please give details. Yes / No – If yes, please give details.	
Fixed Assets	Please provide a full inventory of equipment, machinery, vehicles, fixtures and fittings and any other assets to be included within the sale. List of any items expressly excluded from the sale where any potential confusion may arise, i.e. the item is located on the business premises, the item is used for business purposes in full or part, the item has been seen by the purchaser and may be assumed to be part of the sale.		
Employees	Please provide an up to date list of staff showing: name, sex, length of service, age, salary, any benefits, notice period and position. Include brief description of duties if not clear from job title or position. Please provide copies of all contractual agreements or statutory particulars of employment issued to employees, self-employed staff or sub-contracts. Are you aware of any liability to, or claim likely to be made by, any current or previously employed director or employee. If so, please provide details. Please specify any issues or barriers that will have an impact on a hand-over, e.g. staff share option scheme.		

Section	Item	Put enclosures or detail notes	✔
Employee Pensions & Benefits	List of all employed directors and employees included within any pension, retirement benefit and health-care or life insurance scheme. Please provide a copy of the trust deed, and rules of every pension or retirement benefit scheme of the company or its subsidiaries. Please provide a copy of the contracting-out certificate, if any, issued under the Social Security Pensions Act 1975. Please provide confirmation in relation to every such scheme that it is approved by the Inland Revenue and that such approval is not under threat of withdrawal and that all employers' contributions under any such scheme have been paid up to date. Have you ever had self-employed contractors working for your business? If so, please provide full details including the basis.		
Charges & Guarantees	Copies of all charges and guarantees or other security given by the Vendor either on behalf of the company or personally in relation to the business, such as leases, bank borrowing etc. Are there any product patents owned by the business or any under licence? If so, please give details. Are there any social trends occurring, or political, that you are aware may have an impact on the business? If so, please identify.		
Commit-ments	Please provide details of all hire purchase, credit sale and leasing agreements relating to the business. Please provide any agreement or arrangement (with trade unions or local branches of such unions or such other bodies) relating to the employment of labour by the business. Provide full particulars of any trade associations of which the business is a member.		

Section	Item	Put enclosures or detail notes	✔
Terms and conditions	Are there any terms of business (also pricing) that you know need to be changed or are being changed?	Yes/No – If yes, please give details.	
	Please provide copies of all standard form terms and conditions of supply and/or standard form terms and conditions of purchase of the business.		
Suppliers	Are any key costs likely to rise in the foreseeable future or known to be rising? If so identify.	Yes/No – If yes, please give details.	
Litigation and Disputes	Please specify in detail the title and name of any litigation (civil or criminal) or arbitration relating to the business.		
	Please specify details of any claim made by or against the business likely to lead to litigation (civil or criminal) or arbitration.		
	Are their any outstanding complaints where litigation is being threatened or seems likely?	Yes/No – If yes, please give details.	
	Is there any legislation in force or due to be in force that may affect your business?	Yes/No – If yes, please give details.	
	Has there ever been any investigation by the revenue or reason to believe investigation may occur?	Yes/No – If yes, please give details.	
Integration issues	Are there any items of equipment or systems that will need to be updated by a purchaser?	Yes/No – If yes, please give details.	
Customers	Please supply a breakdown of your turnover by key customer. (Please note all customers who contribute more than 5% of turnover must be identified.) Full details of this information will not be passed to purchasers.		
	Are your customers on contract? If so, are there any due for renewal? If not, are there any letters exchanging terms of business? If so, please identify.	Yes/No – If yes, please give details.	
	Are there any discount arrangements with customers? If so, please identify.	Yes/No – If yes, please give details.	
	Are you aware of any key suppliers that may need to be tackled prior to sale? If so, please provide details.		

Section	Item	Put enclosures or detail notes	✔
Customers	Have you any reason to suspect that any key customers may not be retained on a hand-over?	Yes/No – If yes, please give details	
	Are there any third party investors or stakeholders who may have a claim on the business?	Yes/No – If yes, please give details	

Vendor's Signature

Print name ________________________________Date

Accountant's Signature

Print name ________________________________Date ______________

Glossary of mergers and acquisitions terms

Glossary of mergers and acquisitions terms

This Glossary is designed to give an understanding of terms commonly used within the corporate finance and mergers and acquisitions fields. With certain words and terms we have detailed the common usage and understanding rather than a literal definition.

Accruals. An allowance made within the account for a charge, expense or liability that is often estimated, as the final amount is not known at the accounting date. An example might be a quarterly bill that has not been invoiced by the time the accounts are prepared.

Acid Test Ratio. Also known as Liquid Ratio. It is a ratio used to assess the liquidity of a company, i.e. the circulating assets less stock to current liabilities. Shown as a percentage. For example, a company with liquid assets of £25k incl stock of 15k and current liabilities of 12k will have a liquid ratio of 25000 – 15000 / 12000 = 0.83 = 83%. The company has 83 pence of liquid assets excluding stock for every £1 of current liabilities.

Administration order. An order of a court to place under administration the affairs of a company in financial difficulties with a view to securing its survival as a going concern. If that is not possible the aim is to achieve a more favourable value for its assets than would be possible via liquidation. While under an administration order, the company is managed by an administrator appointed by the court.

Administrative receiverships. Usually appointed to companies by debenture holders, mainly High Street banks, to realize assets by the sale of the business or otherwise to pay the secured creditor. Acting as an agent of the company the administrative receiver has the power to keep the company trading and later sell on its business as a going concern, leaving behind the liabilities.

Aged debtor analysis. A breakdown of the length of time the debts of a business have been outstanding. This would usually be expressed as the amount of debt that has been due for less than 30 days, between 30 and 60 days, between 60 and 90 days and longer than 90 days. This assessment is often used for estimating future cash flow requirements and as part of a business's credit control process.

AIM. Alternative Investment Market. A market of the London Stock Exchange that allows smaller companies to raise capital and have their shares traded in a market without the expense of a full market listing.

Amortization. The process used to treat as an expense the amount in one year deemed to waste away from the value of a fixed asset (usually an intangible fixed asset such as a lease or goodwill). In the USA this is another word for depreciation.

Assets. Any object tangible or intangible owned by a company, including items that it is owed. Current assets include cash, investments, money due, materials and inventories. Fixed assets include land, buildings and machinery. Intangible assets include goodwill.

Asset based finance. Lending that is founded on specific assets, i.e. commercial mortgages based on property. It is often a crucial element when financing a buy-out.

Asset cover. A ratio measuring the solvency of a company. It is calculated by dividing the net assets by the debt.

Audited Financial Statements. The financial statements of a business prepared by a registered auditor and qualified accountant in accordance with general accounting principles. These statements show the business's financial position and the results of its operations.

Balance sheet. A statement presenting the status of the business's assets, liabilities and equity on a given date.

Bankruptcy. Technically this only relates to personal insolvency under the supervision of the Court. It is a phrase, however, that lay people often misapply to corporate insolvency too.

Bear. A dealer or speculator on the stock exchange, currency market or commodity market who expect prices to fall.

Bear market. One in which a dealer or speculator is more likely to sell than to buy. A bear may even sell securities, currencies or goods without having them. This is known as selling short or establishing a bear position. The bear hopes to close (or cover) a short position by buying at a lower price the securities, currencies or goods previously sold. The difference represents the bear's successful profit. A concerted effort to force prices down by one or more bears is known as a bear raid.

Best advice. Seven LAWS of best advice in order of use:

1. Diligently obtain the full facts from a client.
2. Check the facts, needs and objectives of the client.
3. Provide clear considered advice within your area of expertise.
4. Advice must be objective (not influenced by your needs).
5. Qualify the reasons why the advice has been given.
6. Advice must be qualified as your opinion.
7. Check the client has understood advice.

BIMBO. The BIMBO is a combination of a management buy-in and a management buy-out. In a BIMBO, key people such as an Investing Chairman, Finance Director or Managing Director are added to an existing management team, perhaps to replace an existing owner or simply just to strengthen the team. This combination can be ideal in that it provides new, backable management together with the knowledge of the existing management team.

Blue chip. Names we all recognize, companies whose products or services we all use.

Book value/net worth. The accounting value of the business or an asset according to financial records and statements.

BPR. Business property relief. Relief from inheritance tax on relevant business assets.

Brand name. A name identifying a particular product, group of products or service. Typically a well-known name that is immediately associated with the appropriate product or service.

Break even point. The amount of money a product or service needs to be sold for to cover the direct costs associated with producing the product or providing the service.

Bull. A dealer or speculator on the stock exchange, currency market or commodity market who expects prices to rise.

Bull market. One in which a dealer or speculator is more likely to be a buyer than a seller even to the extent of buying without having made a corresponding sale thus establishing a bull position.

Business Angel or Informal Investor. A high net worth individual willing to provide a company with capital in exchange for a high proportion of shares. They will usually fund sums below £250,000. Business angels will often require an exit route. They will normally want a say in the way that the business is run.

Business plan. A detailed plan setting out the objectives of the business over a stated period, often three, five or ten years. For new businesses it is an essential document for raising capital or loans. The plan should include a cash flow analysis, anticipated profit and loss accounts and production figures for at least the first two years. The plan must also include the strategy and tactics which the business intends to use to achieve its objectives.

Buy and Build. Buying a company with a financial and business plan to develop the company significantly in the short and medium term.

Called up share capital. The amount of the issued share capital of a company for which payment has been requested (called up). Some shares are paid for in part, for example an allotment, with subsequent calls for payment. When all calls have been paid the called up share capital will equal the fully paid-up share capital.

Capital. The total sum that an individual has invested in a business or the business net worth.

Capital allowances. Tax relief for capital expenditure given against income on eligible fixed assets similar to depreciation but at set rates pre-determined by the Revenue.

CGT. Capital Gains Tax. Tax payable by an individual on the profit made on the disposal of an asset.

City code on take-overs & mergers. First laid out in 1968 and since modified. The code attempts to ensure all shareholders including minority ones are treated equally, are kept advised of the terms of all bids and counter bids. Its many recommendations are aimed at preventing directors acting in their own interest rather than those of the shareholders to ensure that negotiations are conducted openly and honestly. Representatives from the London Stock Exchange, clearing banks and others compiled the code.

Collateral. A form of security such as shares offered to secure a loan.

Comfort letter. A letter of reassurance from the parent company of a subsidiary trying to borrow money from a bank. The letter will support the application but not act as a guarantee for the loan.

Company voluntary arrangement. Such formal agreements involve the company coming to an arrangement with its creditors to avoid liquidation. The creditors may vote to accept in full settlement a payment less than their rightful due. Upon fulfilment of this arrangement the company can resume business as before. A qualified insolvency practitioner must be appointed to supervise the arrangement.

Completion accounts. A set of financial accounts (principally the balance sheet although usually includes a profit and loss account) produced at the date a business is sold. The completion accounts are produced to show the state of a business at the point of sale. The sale price is often adjusted in accordance with pre-defined formulas applied to the completion accounts.

Compulsory liquidation. This type of liquidation is where an insolvent company is wound up by order of the High Court or County Court with bankruptcy jurisdiction. Either the Official Receiver and/or an outside liquidator deals with the administration of winding up the company's affairs.

Concession. Where a party backs down or agrees to the other party on terms. Concessions are often sought to alleviate deadlocks. In a win/win deal a concession is usually made on both sides to secure a deal.

Confidentiality undertaking. An undertaking provided by a purchasing party to keep all information regarding the business in the strictest confidence. The undertaking is legally binding with recourse. Also known as a non-disclosure agreement (NDA).

Consideration. Proceeds received or receivable on a disposal of an asset. This can be in various forms including cash, shares or loan notes.

Contingent liabilities. An accounting term for a liability that is anticipated if a particular event occurs. In business sales a typical example of where this term might arise is if a Court case is pending at the point of sale. You would calculate the potential loss to the company (contingent liability) if it lost the case. Often in a business sale an indemnity will be asked for from the Vendor against potential contingent liabilities.

Cost of sales. The costs directly associated with providing a product or service. This could be the cost of purchasing the product to sell, or manufacturing a product. The cost of sales does not include overheads such as administration costs, establishment costs or finance costs.

Creditors. Parties that a business owes money to.

Creditors voluntary liquidation. The winding up of a company by special resolution of the members when it is insolvent. This is the most common type of insolvency. The company is wound up outside the jurisdiction of the Court. The procedure must not be confused with Members Voluntary Liquidation where creditors are likely to be paid in full.

CT. Corporation tax. A tax on the profits of a company. Different rates are used for different levels of profits.

Current assets. Cash or assets that are easily converted to cash in a relatively short period of time (no more than one year). They include stock and debtors.

Current liabilities. Short-term liabilities that need to be met in a relatively short period of time (no more that one year). They might include trade creditors, staff salaries, VAT etc.

Data-room. A service made available to both the purchaser and their advisors in order for them to view / inspect company information during the due diligence procedure.

Deadlock. Where parties seek to resolve a conflict or difference but can't see a way. Often deadlock occurs because of a lack of understanding over each party's requirements.

Deal. When the parties involved in a sale have agreed the price and terms under which the transaction is to be carried out.

Debentures. A long-term loan taken out by a company. It is usually repayable by a fixed date. Most debentures carry a fixed rate of interest that must be paid before dividends are paid to the shareholders. Most debentures are secured by the borrower's assets, although some, naked debentures or unsecured debentures are not.

Debtors. Parties that owe money to a business.

Deferred consideration. An agreement in which payment of the consideration is delayed until a certain date or until a specified event has occurred. Often paid in instalments with interest. A vendor loan is a deferred consideration payment. Security and or personal guarantees will often/should be asked to give collateral for deferred payments. See performance related payment.

De-grouping. This is where a company who was a member of a group no longer fulfils the criteria to be a member of the group and therefore exits the group.

De-merger. A company splits up into more than one company. There is a strict legal process to follow.

Depreciation. An accounting method of spreading the cost of a fixed asset over its theoretical useful life within the profit and loss account. When a business purchases a fixed asset, the cost and the value of the asset are usually represented in the balance sheet. The value of the asset is then reduced (depreciated) annually using one of accepted accounting methods of depreciation, and the depreciation is shown in the profit and loss account with the reduced value of the asset being shown in the balance sheet.

Dilapidations. Repairs required reinstating a leasehold property back to its original state and condition on the expiry or termination of a lease.

Director loans. A loan made by the director of a company to the company or from the company to a director of the company. There are strict rules governing director loans. Typically director loans are seen in privately owned companies where the shareholders are the directors.

Director remuneration (emoluments). The amounts paid to the directors of a company in the form of salaries, pension contributions and other forms of benefits in respect of fulfilling the role of a director and performing the duties of office.

Disclosure letter & disclosure bundle. A document disclosing statements of condition, fact and Vendor's beliefs relating to a business at the time of sale. It forms part of the completion documentation. A disclosure letter serves two purposes. One is to attach a set of all relevant company documentation and the second is to vary the effect of the warranties contained in a Sale and Purchase Agreement. A good example in a business sale might be 'not all PC software is licensed. Copies of licensees thus far held.'

Discounted cash flow. A method of budgeting that estimates today's value of money to be received in the future; it is discounted due to the uncertainty of its true value in the future and for the cost of the capital (less valuable than the cash in your hand today).

Dividend. Distributions to shareholders of a company out of post-tax retained profits.

Dividend cover. Dividend cover is the number of times that a company's dividends could be paid out of its net profit after tax in the same period (post tax net profit divided by the dividends paid). Prudent companies retain a percentage of their earnings. A ratio of 2 or more is generally accepted as comfortable, and anything below 1? as an alarm bell. If the ratio sinks below 1, the company is paying out more than its earnings and distributing part of its retained surpluses. Circumstances vary – this may or may not be a bad thing in the shorter term. However, it is clearly a situation which cannot continue indefinitely.

Dividend yield. The dividend yield is one of the key measurements for shareholders. This is the amount of dividend received per share expressed as a percentage of the market price of the share. The dividend may be paid in two instalments: the interim and final dividends. Most dividends are paid after deduction of tax: yields are generally expressed 'gross'. The tax deducted is added back as part of the calculation. A gross yield of 4 per cent is equivalent to a net yield of 2.4 per cent to a 40 per cent taxpayer.

How should we interpret the yield?

Very high yields may indicate that a company was expected to reduce its dividend pay out. The share price has fallen on the stock market because reduced profits are expected. The calculation uses last year's dividend and this year's (reduced) share price. Last year's dividend is expected to have been higher than this year's.

Low yields may indicate expectations both of a growth in profits and of increased dividends and a share price, which has already risen. Shares in different companies may be compared through dividend yields.

Due diligence. Due diligence is the process prior to completing and acquisition, of verifying the information provided and diligently checking the suitability of the acquisition, the company's history and future prospects. External professional advisors are often used to assist in this process. Due diligence is sometimes broken down into a number of distinct areas; financial, legal, commercial, environmental, cultural, IT etc.

EBITDA. Earnings before interest, tax, depreciation and amortization.

EBITD. Earnings before interest, tax, depreciation.

EBIT. Earnings before interest, tax.

Earn out. Where some or all of the purchase price for a business is paid over a period of time. This usually involves a continued involvement from the Vendor and may also be a variable sum, linked to certain criteria being met, typically the future financial performance of the business.

Economy of scale. Where the linking of two operations provides a direct cost saving enabling enhanced operating profits. Typically, with an acquisition, this is where the two businesses' functions may duplicate each other. The closure or scaling down of one creates better economies, i.e. reduces costs creating more profit.

EIS. Enterprise Investment Scheme. Tax efficient investment in a company for individuals enabling either income tax relief and/ or reinvestment relief for capital gains tax purposes. There are strict conditions applying to the investor, the investment and the company. The company equivalent is the corporate venturing scheme.

Elevator deal. A transaction with a significant shareholding purchased, but probably less than 50% by a company willing/wishing to invest in a venture to grow it. The remaining element is retained by the existing shareholders who stay with the business and use the funds (and probably infrastructure/ideas) of the investor to grow. As the business grows the investor has the right to buy the remaining element at a higher 'elevated' price, usually predetermined by formula.

Employment taxes. Tax payable by an employer on earnings of employees. It includes Pay As You Earn (PAYE) and National Insurance Contributions (NIC).

Equity. The amount by which the value of an asset exceeds any liabilities attached to it.

Equity finance. A form of finance, where equity in the business is provided in return for providing finance.

Escrow. Noun – Law – 'a bond, deed, deposit kept by a neutral third party until a specified condition has been fulfilled'.

Origin; old French (legal system has origins in France) – 'escroe' meaning 'scrap, scroll'. Related to 'shred' and, therefore, 'shroud'.

Shroud – length of cloth or enveloping garment or a thing that obscures or protective casing concealing from view.

Example: A deed that has been signed but will not become operative until a pre-determined event takes place. Money held in escrow is controlled by a third party (often a lawyer) and is only released to the beneficiaries when a certain event takes place (usually completion).

Factoring. The buying of trade debts of a company assuming the task of debt collection and accepting the credit risk, thus providing the company with working capital. A firm that engages in factoring is called a factor.

Financial assistance. Section 151 of the Companies Act specifies that no company can financially assist in the purchase of its own shares. The act aims to protect any company from exhausting its own capital base and thus compromising its ability to meet any liabilities to its creditors. See 'Whitewash'.

Financial reporting for smaller entities. The reporting standards for businesses have been revised and updated in several areas. Accountants are required to prepare them according to published financial reporting standards. These set out the permitted methods of accounting for certain transactions and situations. These standards have to cover all sorts of issues that are sometimes only relevant to larger companies. As a result, there is now a separate, less complex, standard for smaller companies and other organizations, known as the Financial Reporting Standard for Smaller Entities, or FRSSE (pronounced 'fruzzy'!). As new standards are issued, the FRSSE is amended to reflect those aspects that apply to smaller companies.

Financial statement. The annual statement summarizing a company's activities over the last year. This includes the profit and loss account, balance sheet and, if required, a cash-flow statement.

Fiscal year. The financial year imposed by the Government for the purposes of assessing tax. It runs from April 6th to April 5th of the following year.

Fixed assets. Assets that are not traded in the course of the normal day to day activities of a business. The nature of the business will usually dictate whether an asset is treated as a fixed asset or a current asset. For example a car would usually be treated as a current asset (stock) by a car dealership (their business is selling cars), whereas a recruitment company would usually list a car as a fixed asset (the car is a tool that helps the business trade, rather than an item which the business trades.)

Fixed asset and goodwill sale. Often referred to incorrectly as an asset and goodwill sale. It means where the fixed assets of a business, its goodwill, customers, staff and know-how are sold on in a way that enables continuance of a business. In the case of a limited company, the company sells its fixed assets and goodwill, however no shares change hands.

Float. A flotation is the offering of initial shares to the public on a quoted stock market. Will it float or sink. For example, will the public buy the offering? The process is known as an initial price offering.

Franchising. Franchiser – an agreement whereby the franchisor (a primary company) provides a market tested business package to another business (the franchisee). The latter then operates under the franchisor's trade name, marketing goods according to an agreed contract and either for a fee or restricted supply chain or similar. Typically a franchisor will allow a number of franchisees to operate the business model, usually restricted by financial territory to prevent competition among the franchisees.

FT-SE. Financial Times Stock Exchange Share Index sometimes known as the Footsie. The Financial Times publishes the FT-SE 100 Share Index, which reflects the combined performance of the 100 largest companies quoted on the stock market. The index shows the current level, the highs and lows, and levels at other specified dates. The FT-SE 250 shows the combined performance of the next 250 largest companies below the top 100. The FT Actuaries All Share Index shows the daily performance of the top 800 companies.

GAAP. Generally Accepted Accounting Principles. An accounting practice whereby your accounts have been prepared in agreement with normal accounting conventions. Please note that there are some differences between UK and American GAAP processes.

Gearing. The level of borrowing (debt) to equity.

Golden handcuffs (loyalty bonus). Financial incentives offered to key staff to persuade them to remain with a business after the sale. Also known as loyalty bonus. Usually paid to non-shareholding key staff if they remain with the business for a defined period after sale or until a pre-defined event occurs.

Goodwill. Goodwill: a kindly feeling, a well-being, benevolence.

What is business goodwill? The advantage or favour a business has in its custom and trade.

What is financial goodwill? The excess of the purchase price (not its valuation but what is achieved) over and above the value assigned to its net assets exclusive of goodwill.

In other words goodwill is an abstract concept. It also means different things to different people. Therefore it stands to reason that goodwill is a matter of opinion. Some even argue that it does not exist. Goodwill could also be the measure of trust the market has in a business.

Grooming. The process of preparing a business for sale in order to make it more attractive to a potential purchaser.

Gross profit. The turnover of a business (total revenue generated) less direct costs (those costs that are directly attributable to the generation of the turnover).

Group. A parent undertaking and its subsidiary or subsidiaries.

Hand-over. A period in which the selling party 'hands-over' knowledge, contacts, relationships etc. to the Purchaser. The complexity of the business being sold, level of involvement in the day-to-day running of the business the Vendor has, and skills and industry experience the Purchaser has will dictate the length and structure of the hand-over required.

Heads of terms. A document outlining the key points of an agreed transaction that is then used as the basis to prepare the legal contracts. The heads of terms is not usually legally binding save for specific clauses relating to exclusivity and confidentiality.

Hive down. Where the trade and assets of a company are transferred into a subsidiary company.

Hive up. Where the trade and assets of a company are transferred into a parent company.

House keeping. Non-productive but necessary procedures typically relating to record keeping and administrative issues. Whilst good house keeping is an important part of all businesses on an ongoing basis, it is often only taken seriously in the period preceding a sale, particularly in the case of small businesses.

IBA. Industrial buildings allowance. Similar to a capital allowance but applied to certain industrial buildings such as factories and warehouses.

IHT. Inheritance tax. Tax levied on certain lifetime transfers and estates on the death of individuals.

Incorporation. The process by which a company is registered under the Companies Act. The formation of an association that has 'corporate identity', i.e. an identity that is distinct from its members.

Indemnities (Warranties and Indemnities). An indemnity is an undertaking to pay or reimburse in full without declaration against a particular event occurring. It is not subject to any minimum or maximum amount. Often money will be held in an account [see escrow] against a financial claim being made against a warranty. A warranty is an undertaking or guarantee offered against a potential event. It may be subject to restrictions on the minimum or maximum amount referred to in the sale and purchase agreement.

Input tax. VAT on purchases from suppliers.

Insolvency. An excess of liabilities over assets and an inability to meet debts as they fall due. This often leads to liquidation although not always.

Intangible assets. Fixed assets that are intangible. Typically goodwill, intellectual property or investments.

Interest relief on borrowings. Tax relief given for interest on loans made by a qualifying individual for the purposes of investing in a qualifying company or partnership.

IPO. Initial Public Offering – also known as flotation.

IPR. Intellectual Property Rights – the right of ownership of intangible property, such as patents, copyrights trademarks etc.

IRR. Internal rate of return.

Know-how. The procedures, ideas, products, vision and personal knowledge of a business normally residing in its people. Unless this is transferred on a sale, goodwill will rapidly dissipate. An experienced buyer will work out a deal that retains know-how.

Large business. Large companies – firms with over 250 employees

Leverage. See 'Gearing'.

Liability. An obligation to transfer economic benefit as a result of past transactions. A contingent liability may or may not become a liability.

Limited company. A limited company is a separate entity from its owners (members, shareholders). Its Directors are not normally liable for its debts although they may be asked to give personal guarantees on certain loans and liabilities. The company must be registered and submit properly prepared statutory financial statements. There are specific rules and regulations governing the way a limited company is set up and run which must be followed.

Listing. The flotation of a company on the stock exchange.

Loan note. The legal document detailing the terms of 'loan capital'; effectively an IOU issued by a company. Loan capital is capital used to finance an organization that is subject to interest over the life of the loan, at the end of which the loan is usually repaid (see Debenture). In M&A terms, a loan note is issued by a purchasing company to the seller in place of cash. From the purchaser's point of view this assists them in the cash flow requirements of an acquisition. From a seller's point of view certain types of loan notes can be tax beneficial, particularly as the taxation is usually crystallized at the time of issue of the loan note, however is not payable until the loan note is realized.

Loss relief. Tax relief for trading or capital losses given by setting losses against taxable income or chargeable gains (individuals) and taxable profits (companies).

Market capitalization. This is the value put on the company by the stock market. It represents the cost of buying all the shares in the company at the share price quoted.

MBI (Management Buy-In). The acquisition of a company by a manager or management team from outside the company who buy it, and then become the new managers.

MBO (Management Buy-Out). The acquisition of a company by its existing managers.

Medium business. A business that can claim two or more of the following:

- Balance sheet not exceeding £5.6m
- Turnover not exceeding £11.2m
- Average number of employees not exceeding 250.

Members voluntary liquidation. In this instance the company must be solvent. The directors are obliged to make a statutory declaration that they have formed the opinion that the company will be able to pay its debts (including the cost of liquidation) in full, together with interest at the official rate, within twelve months. The burden of proof is on the directors.

Memorandum of Association. An official document setting out a company's existence. It includes the registered office of the company. A statement of the company's objectives (called the objects clause), the amount of authorized share capital and its division.

Merger. A combination of two or more businesses on an equal footing that results in the creation of a new reporting entity. The shareholders of the combining entities mutually share the risks and rewards of the new entity. (Approval of the monopolies and mergers commission may be required.) For publicly quoted companies mergers must be conducted on lines sanctioned by the City code on take-overs and mergers.

Micro-firms. Firms with fewer than 9 employees.

Minority shareholder. A shareholder who holds less than 50 % of the company's shares is classed as a minority shareholder. They can receive their share of the profits in the form of dividends however they cannot on their own control or determine company policies.

Negotiation. The process of trying to bring together two or more parties in order that an agreement is reached. Generally the aim of negotiation is to obtain a mutually beneficial solution, which involves dovetailing interests giving both sides a degree of satisfaction to the agreement.

Win/Win: Where both sides feel they have obtained a good deal.

Win/Lose: Where one side is feeling they have a good deal and the other feels hard done by. The deal might still happen but there will be bad feeling that might result in criticism, or lack of support in a hand-over.

Lose/Lose: Where ultimately neither side succeeds in their objectives. This might occur when a Win/Lose deal is agreed and one party backs out leaving both with large professional bills.

Net asset value. The value of the assets of the company plus what it is owed minus what it owes. Shown as shareholders' funds on a balance sheet.

Net profit. The amount of income earned by an organization after deducting all relevant costs and expenditure.

Net return. This is the true economic view of a company. It is calculated by recasting the financial statements of a business to eliminate direct and indirect owner-related expenses as well as extraordinary or non-recurring items. This type of recast is known as an add-back. There might also be the converse, an add-on where the expenses are not realistic with beneficial rents or lower salaries being paid.

Non-Embarrassment Clause. The rights given to a vendor should a successful purchaser re-sell the business within a certain period of time and who benefits from a higher sale value. This usually takes the form of financial compensation.

Ofex. (Of-exchange) An independent market for listing small to medium sized companies. Now known as PLUS.

Open Market Value. How much an asset will fetch if sold on the open market.

OTT – Option to Tax. The ability of a purchaser/ owner of a commercial property to elect for the property to be subject to VAT by waiving the usual VAT exempt status in order to recover VAT input tax.

Output tax. VAT charged by a vendor on its supplies to its customers.

Partnership. A partnership involves two or more people jointly running a business with a view to making a profit. Although you do not have to formally register a partnership, it is recommended that a Partnership Agreement be drawn up. Included in the agreement should be who has put what into the business, who does what work, how your profits are shared and what would happen if you decided to wind up the partnership. Each partner is personally liable for all debts incurred by the business. Trust in this type of business relationship is therefore crucial.

Payback period. How long it will take to repay the amount invested at current levels of earning.

Perception value. Perception value is denominated by the market view of a business. This can be measured by market comparison. Literally what others are selling for but also instinct. The most common measure of this perception value is the selection of a profit earnings ratio (a P/E multiple). (In its inverse state this is called ROCE, return on capital employed.)

Performance related payment. Where part of the consideration for the purchase of a business is deferred until a later date and is linked to the future performance of the business. Similar to deferred payments and earn outs.

PEST. A management or valuation technique where an analysis of the environmental forces that effect a business is created. A review of national and global trends:

- Political
- Economic
- Social or sociological
- Technical

Phoenix. A buy-out from a liquidator.

Preparation. This is where all parties research, consider, brainstorm and assess prior to transactions. A good negotiator can never do too much preparation.

Price. The monetary value that a business is marketed for sale.

Price earnings ratio (P/E) ratio. The P/E ratio is the ratio of the price paid per share in a company to the earnings that share produces annually.

For a quoted company this is calculated as the current quoted share price divided by the year-end dividend declared per share.

For privately owned companies this is more likely to be the price paid per share divided by the post-tax profit per share.

The P/E ratio is widely quoted as a basis for comparison. There are those who regard P/E ratios as having their uses, even if they are a limited tool. Different types of businesses attract different P/E ratios.

Put option. The right to buy or sell a defined number of shares at a pre-agreed price at a particular date. This is sometimes used if a purchaser buys a proportion of a business and has a put option to buy more of it at a later date.

R&D (Research & Development). The investigation undertaken to gain new scientific or technical knowledge and understanding, and/or the use of scientific or technical knowledge to produce new or substantially improved materials, devises, products, processes, systems or services prior to commencement of commercial production.

Accounting standards distinguish between pure research, applied research and development. Depending on the category or R&D, the costs can either be written off against tax immediately, or capitalized and amortized.

Redundancy. Where an organization no longer has a commercial use for some of its functions, the staff that perform those functions may be made redundant and receive a redundancy payment. There are very strict rules governing redundancy. The statutory calculations for redundancy payments can be found on the following web site:

http://www.dti.gov.uk/cgi-bin/er_reconner.pl

Restriction of trade (non-competition clause). A clause or series of clauses in a sale contract that prevents the seller from entering into a competitive business or performing competitive activities after the sale of a business. Typically the restrictions will be before a defined period and within a defined geographical area. Unlike employment law where restrictive covenants imposed on employees are often considered unenforceable, they are enforceable in the case of the sale of a business when drafted correctly.

Return on capital employed (R.O.C.E.). An accounting ratio expressing the profit of an organization as a percentage of the capital employed (the rate of return required on money invested). This should certainly be more than the rate of interest you could get from leaving your money in a building society account. This is the reverse ratio of a P/E ratio.

Roll-over tax relief. Relief from capital gains tax (or corporation tax on chargeable gains) on eligible disposals. The financial gain from the disposal of an asset may be deferred if the proceeds are used to purchase another qualifying asset. Strict rules apply to roll-over relief and what is accepted as a qualifying asset.

Sale and Purchase Agreement (SPA). A legal contract setting out the details and terms of the purchase of a business or business asset. This is typically drawn up by lawyers and includes details of all aspects of the transaction, including details of what is being sold, the price to be paid, any restrictive covenants on both buying and selling parties and warranties and indemnities provided to the purchaser by the seller etc.

Schedule of staff. A comprehensive list of all staff, their job description, their addresses, the length of their employment, their salaries and benefits and any outstanding holidays.

Schedule 22 employment taxes. Tax and NIC payable by either an employer and/ or the employee where shares or share options are transferred to an employee at an undervalue. There are special rules relating to MBOs.

Section 320. Provisions in the Companies Act that prevents a director purchasing more than 10% of the company's net assets without obtaining permission from the shareholders.

Securities and Futures Authority (SFA). The self-regulating authority responsible for regulating the conduct of brokers and dealers in securities, options and futures.

Security. An asset or loan to which a lender can have recourse if a borrower defaults on his loan payments. Sometimes referred to as collateral or a charge.

Shares. Shares are equal parts into which the capital stock of a company is divided. They fall into two basic categories:

1 Ordinary shares

2 Preference shares

When we buy shares, we are investing in the future performance of the company, which originally issued them. We are looking for income (received via dividend payments) or capital gain (received if we sell shares at a higher price than we paid for them) or both.

Shares – ordinary. Companies sometimes subdivide their ordinary shares into different classes, e.g. to reflect different dates of issue. Ordinary shares are securities issued by companies in return for the investment of risk capital. The risk is high because the claims of owners of ordinary shares rank behind those of all others in the event of the company being wound up and its income and assets distributed.

Limited liability: here, the shareholders' risk is limited to the value of the ordinary shares. If the business fails their liability for losses incurred by creditors and lenders is limited to the funds they have invested in the business – hence the term 'limited liability company'.

Potential for gain: to compensate for their high risk status, ordinary shares offer unlimited potential for gain because other forms of capital, e.g. preference shares have strictly limited claims on the income and assets of the business.

Shareholders' rights: ordinary shareholders also have voting rights on a whole range of issues. The exercise of these rights by an individual shareholder may be of limited significance. This is particularly so where institutional investors, e.g. insurance companies own very large blocks of shares.

Shares – preference. Preference shares provide part of the equity capital of a company. They carry very limited rights of ownership, restricted often to the right to vote if preference dividends remain unpaid. In reality, preference shares are a form of specialized debt. They carry rights to:

- A fixed interest rate rather than dividends.
- Repayment of the par value of the share in the event of winding up. Preference shareholders rank behind unsecured creditors and ahead of ordinary shareholders.

Share price. The share price: For publicly quoted companies, this is usually the previous day's closing mid-market price in pence (i.e. halfway between the offer and bid price at the previous day's close of business) or the price change from the previous trading day.

Highest and lowest prices: These are the share's maximum and minimum prices over the prior 52-week period.

Share transfer. A change in the ownership of a share or stock.

Skeletons in the cupboard. Hidden liabilities (see contingent liabilities) normally referred to as ones that have been left dusty, ignored or hidden.

Small businesses. Firms with between 10 – 49 employees.

SMEs. Small to medium sized enterprises.

Sole trader. To become a 'sole trader', all you need to do is inform the Income Tax and Social Security authorities that you want to work for yourself. You have the freedom to choose how you do things and in many ways your business will be relatively simple to manage, even the book keeping and accounting should be straightforward. You are, however, responsible and liable for every aspect of your business and if things do go wrong, your personal possessions as well as your business may be at risk.

Solvency. A business with the ability to meet its financial obligations.

SSE. Substantial shareholding exemption. Corporation tax exemption given to trading companies disposing of a greater than 10% interest in another trading company from corporation tax on chargeable gains.

Stamp duty. A ?% duty on documents relating to the purchase or transfer of shares and securities. These must be physically stamped at a Stamp Office and the duty paid to the Revenue.

Stamp duty land tax. A tax paid by the buyer on the acquisition of land and/ or property. Separate rates apply to outright purchases and to leases. See www.inlandrevenue.gov.uk for rates.

Subsidiary. A company controlled by a parent or holding company.

Summarizing. Verbally and then preferably in writing outlining the terms or agreements to date in a way that sets out the clear progress.

Sweetheart approach. A 'one' company direct approach. They are quick and easy deals but with no competitive process often leading to lower values.

SWOT. An analysis tool identifying:

- Strengths
- Weaknesses
- Opportunities
- Threats

Synergy. Where a buyer is able to gain added profits out of an existing business by linking their own operation and sharing knowledge or resource. A good example is where clients in existing operations can be crossed over. It is not an economy of scale, which is where profits can be enhanced by a direct reduction in costs by reducing the 'scale' of the two linked operations.

Taper relief. A relief given against the capital gains tax payable on the sale of an asset, based on the type of asset and the qualifying period of ownership. Relief for business assets is more substantial than for non-business assets. Taper relief is not available on disposals by companies.

Types of business asset (current definitions):

- Shares in a trading company not listed on the Stock Exchange
- Shares in a trading company in which the individual has power to exercise at least 5% of the voting rights

- Shares in a trading company in which the individual works full or part time
- Shares in any company in which the individual is an employee or director and has less than 10% of the shares
- Assets owned by an individual and used by the individual either in his business or in his partnership
- Assets owned by an individual and used by a qualifying company
- Assets owned by an individual and used for the purposes of his employment
- Assets owned by individuals and used for trade purposes (e.g. commercial investment property).

Non-business assets:

- Asset that does not satisfy the definition of a business asset
- The Revenue has issued guidance on the interpretation of trading companies. Inland Revenue literature order line 0645 000404 Inland Revenue help desk 0645 000444.

Target. The chosen company to be acquired.

Tax rates. Different rates of tax apply to different taxes, to different sources of income and/ or depending on whether the taxpayer is an individual, a company or other entity (e.g. trust). Current tax rates can be viewed on the Revenue website www.hmrc.gov.uk.

Trade losses. Losses made in normal trade of business.

Trade purchaser. An industrial buyer of companies.

Troubleshoot the deal. To look ahead and pre-empt potential problems in deal. If you know these issues you are then prepared to:

- Hurdle them with solutions.
- Go around them.
- Bring them out in the open.
- Ignore them.

Third Party referral. Where a third party needs to be referred to in certain decision-making processes. This is sometimes used as a negotiating tactic, by giving the impression that certain decisions are beyond one party's control.

TOGC – Transfer of a going concern. Relates to the transfer of a business as a going concern whereby the seller does not charge VAT on stock, assets, goodwill etc and the purchaser does not claim input tax.

TUPE – Transfer of Undertakings (Protection of Employment) Regulations 1981. Regulations governing the right of employees to have continuous employment and have their terms of employment honoured and maintained when business activities are transferred from one party to another. This is applicable to whole businesses or divisions of businesses.

One misconception of purchasers particularly in an asset sale is that they can leave behind unwanted employees. However, all employees are covered by TUPE and as a result of the business being transferred as a going concern and classified as an 'undertaking', they will automatically become employed by the purchaser.

In addition, the accrued rights and claims and terms and conditions will pass to the purchaser. As many acquisitions lead to rationalization of workforce it is essential that the purchaser quantifies the total contingent liability prior to the transaction and it is made clear that this is his/her responsibility. The purchaser should insist on warranties and indemnities with respect to employee claims and attaching contingent liabilities.

USP. Unique selling point. Something relating to the product or service which a business provides that differentiates it from the competition.

Valuation. This is the calculated estimated value of a business. To value a business it is necessary to understand its structure. The type of business, the way in which it is run and trades affects the mathematical calculations that are used in assessing its value.

There are four elements that should be considered when determining a value: property, other fixed assets, net current assets and goodwill. Two examples of property are freehold and leasehold; in very broad terms the first has a value the second usually does not. Other fixed assets include such items as fixtures and fittings, plant, equipment and vehicles that should be valued on a second hand resale basis. Net current assets including items such as stock, cash, debtor/creditor balance etc. have a value at cost to the business with old or redundant stock being discounted or written off. Goodwill is the intangible element that has a value reflecting historical trading patterns, future potential and the businesses financial results. To ascertain the value of goodwill a multiplier is often used on both the visible and invisible profits of the business.

The worth of a business is a combined value of the above. But before the four elements are simply added up a consideration has to be made between the total investment level and profits achieved. If one of the first three elements that make up the price is unusually high, it may have a detrimental effect on the goodwill element. This is determined by using a lower multiplier when calculating the goodwill. Once all factors have been considered the business then has a calculated value.

Valuations and FRSSE (Financial Reporting for Smaller Entities). Recent revisions in the reporting standards for limited companies, which comprise small businesses, include some new rules, especially in the area of goodwill. They require purchased goodwill and intangible assets to be depreciated over their useful economic life and in any case over a period not exceeding 20 years. In certain situations, where the value of fixed assets or capitalized goodwill is impaired, (for example as a result of obsolescence or a fall in demand for a product) the impairment must recognize immediately in the financial statements.

The effect of FRSSE on valuations is that it down values businesses likely to appeal to PLCs and arguably although normally increases the value to private individuals owning over the long term. FRSSE appears to work alongside the Taper relief concept. You depreciate your goodwill over 20 years. Your tax relief appreciates when selling over 10 years??

VAT. Value Added Tax. A transaction tax payable when a taxable person makes a taxable supply of goods or services in the course of business. There are a number of rates.

Venture Capitalist or VC. A person or a firm investing funds in a higher than usual risk business venture expecting high financial returns.

Warranties (Warranties and Indemnities). A warranty is an undertaking or guarantee offered against a potential event. It may be subject to restrictions on the minimum or maximum amount referred to in the sale and purchase agreement. An indemnity is an undertaking to pay or reimburse in full without declaration against a particular event occurring. It is not subject to any minimum or maximum amount. Often money will be held in an account [see escrow] against a financial claim being made against a warranty.

Whitewash. See Financial Assistance

Whitewashing is the procedure authorized by the Companies Act in order for a company to assist in the purchase of its own shares. This is only permitted should a company be able to prove that it can pay its debt for a period of 12 months following the assistance being given. There are strict rules governing the whitewash procedure that must be followed.

Working capital. Readily accessible capital available for the day-to-day running of a business. In accounting reports this is calculated as the current assets minus current liabilities.

Yellow Book. Another name for the 'Admission of Securities to Listing'. A book issued by the Council of the London Stock Exchange that sets out the regulations for admission to the Official List and the obligations of companies with listed securities.